2000 MOST COMMON JAPANESE WORDS IN CONTEXT

Get Fluent & Increase Your Japanese
Vocabulary with 2000 Japanese Phrases

Japanese Language Lessons

Free Book Reveals The 6 Step Blueprint That Took Students
<u>From Language Learners To Fluent In 3 Months</u>

- **6 Unbelievable Hacks** that will accelerate your learning curve
- **Mind Training:** why memorizing vocabulary is easy
- **One Hack To Rule Them All:** This <u>secret nugget</u> will blow you away...

Head over to **<u>LingoMastery.com/hacks</u>**
and claim your free book now!

CONTENTS

INTRODUCTION

Congratulations for getting "2000 Most Common Japanese Words in Context"! You made a big step towards achieving a native-like proficiency.

We all know that the best way to learn a foreign language is to live in the country where the language is spoken. However, it's not always possible for most people with jobs, schools, and family. That is why this book is assembled to give you the ultimate experience as if you are living in Japan. This book presents expressions and phrases in an order based on frequency in both spoken and written language. Therefore, the ones listed at the top are the words you would hear if you had just arrived on the streets of Japan.

When you are learning a language while being a foreign country you would normally resort to following a textbook that teaches you basic grammar rules, and perhaps looking up dictionaries for the meaning of words. In that manner, you only learn the words you look up. There are over a half million words in Japanese dictionaries. It would take over 100 years for you if you learnt 10 words a day. This book helps you accelerate that process to 6 months or so, depending on how many words you can attempt to learn each day.

One of the things you might attempt when learning a foreign language is to make friends who speak the language and learn from conversations with them. While it is highly recommended, what could be left out is the written language. In order to improve fluency, you will need to know the written language as well, and some words or phrases may only appear in writing. This book is comprised of frequently appearing words in both spoken and written Japanese.

This book is particularly useful for those people who have spent some time studying Japanese, and have some understanding of the grammar, but find it difficult to use the learned language in actual situations. When you master these 2000 words and phrases you will be comfortable with not just living in or visiting Japan, but also attending schools or having a business conversation with a native Japanese speaker.

Five reasons why this book will help you boost your Japanese proficiency:

1. As words are listed by frequency in both spoken and written usage, you will have the same experience as if you are learning to them in Japan.

- The ones listed at the top are the words that are most frequently used, and that you may hear if you have just arrived on the streets of Japan.
- The 2000 useful words and phrases reoccur in the sample sentences like in real conversations. Even if you did not master a word the first time, you will have a chance to see it in other phrases and become familiar with it. For your optimal learning experience, the sentences gradually get more complex; using the words that have appeared before.

2. Useful and practical expressions and phrases for real living or visiting.

- Though this book is not a travel guide, it is a great resource for real situations, such as asking directions, shopping, housing, school, workplace or emergency calling.

- Sample sentences depict common social situations in Japan. You will get an insight of life in Japan, as you would by reading newspapers or watching TV news.

3. Both conversational and written Japanese.

- Includes greeting phrases that people actually use. Just like you wouldn't necessarily start a conversation with "How do you do?", there are a variety of phrases other than *Konnichiwa*.
- Includes a variety of frequently used interjections. Almost every conversational phrase has an interjection in real conversations. Sometimes, a great deal of communication can be achieved by knowing and using interjections, like saying "Wow!", "Err", "Oh…" or "Hmm…".
- Each word or phrase is shown in the most commonly used combination of hiragana, katakana and kanji. Some phrases are only written with hiragana while others are more frequently written in kanji. Japanese students are taught hiragana and katakana in the first grade in elementary school, but their kanji learning follow the next 10 years or more. This book cuts 10 years of learning time by showing the most general combinations of the three.

4. More than a grammar book.

- Includes frequently used particles along with sample sentences. Particles may be one of the most difficult aspects of language. Unlike nouns or verbs, dictionaries merely explain briefly, or present too many variations, only to confuse you. This book presents commonly used particles in an orderly manner, and by going through the book, you can naturally familiarize yourself with the way they are used in the Japanese language.

- Great supplement for studying for the JLPT or other Japanese language tests. Though this book is not intended as test prep, you can learn words and phrases for general topics in everyday situations, and even some simple critiques. These are some of the things particularly important for proficiency tests but hard to learn from grammar books.

5. Modern and traditional culture

- Japan is a farming country with four seasons. There are cultural rituals and holidays associated with the seasons throughout the year. In this book traditional rituals for all seasons are introduced in sample sentences, such as *Hinamatsuri* (doll festival for girls) in March or *Koinobori* (carp fish flag festival) in May.
- Includes foreign borrowed words that have become an essential part of modern Japanese language. Some words have the same vowels and syllables, like pi-a-no for piano, while others have switched vowels, like e-a-ro-bi-ku-su for aerobics.
- Includes foreign country names in the order of frequency, topped with USA and England as well as France and Italy.

How to use this book:

Following a **list number,** each word is presented with **most appropriate Japanese written characters/English phonology** [the abbreviated part of speech] *English meaning,* then a sample sentence in Japanese and the English translation.

(Sample)

1077- 緑/midori [n] *green*

信号は緑色なのに青信号と呼ばれます。
Although traffic lights are **green**, they are called blue lights.

4

For English phonology, the revised Hepburn Romanization system is used, with an exception for long vowels. Long vowels are shown with a non-Hepburn Romanization that is authorized by the Japanese Foreign Ministry.

This chart shows the <u>Romanization</u> used in this book with each corresponding hiragana.

a	あ	i	い	u	う	e	え	o	お
ka	か	ki	き	ku	く	ke	け	ko	こ
sa	さ	shi	し	su	す	se	せ	so	そ
ta	た	chi	ち	tsu	つ	te	て	to	と
na	な	ni	に	nu	ぬ	ne	ね	no	の
ha	は	hi	ひ	fu	ふ	he	へ	ho	ほ
ma	ま	mi	み	mu	む	me	め	mo	も
ya	や			yu	ゆ			yo	よ
ra	ら	ri	り	ru	る	re	れ	ro	ろ
wa	わ							wo	を
n	ん								
n'	ん	(an apostrophe is used when the ん character is followed by a vowel or a y)							
wa	は	(particle)							
ga	が	gi	ぎ	gu	ぐ	ge	げ	go	ご
za	ざ	ji	じ	zu	ず	ze	ぜ	zo	ぞ
da	だ	ji	ぢ	zu	づ	de	で	do	ど
ba	ば	bi	び	bu	ぶ	be	べ	bo	ぼ
pa	ぱ	pi	ぴ	pu	ぷ	pe	ぺ	po	ぽ
kya	きゃ			kyu	きゅ			kyo	きょ
sha	しゃ			shu	しゅ			sho	しょ
cha	ちゃ			chu	ちゅ			cho	ちょ
nya	にゃ			nyu	にゅ			nyo	にょ

5

hya	ひゃ			hyu	ひゅ			hyo	ひょ
mya	みゃ			myu	みゅ			myo	みょ
rya	りゃ			ryu	りゅ			ryo	りょ
gya	ぎゃ			gyu	ぎゅ			gyo	ぎょ
ja	じゃ			ju	じゅ			jo	じょ
bya	びゃ			byu	びゅ			byo	びょ
pa	ぱ	pi	ぴ	pu	ぷ	pe	ぺ	po	ぽ
pya	ぴゃ			pyu	ぴゅ			pyo	ぴょ
aa	ああ	ii	いい	uu	うう	ee	ええ	oo	おお
								ou	おう

Here is a reference for abbreviated parts of speech.

[adn] adnominal

[adv] adverb

[aux] auxiliary

[conj] conjunction

[cp] compound

[i-adj] i-adjective

[interj] interjection

[n] noun

[na-adj] na-adjective

[num] numeral

[p] particle

[p. case] case particle

[p. conj] conjunctive particle

[p. dic] discourse particle

[pron] pronoun

[v] verb

Enjoy the experience as you learn Japanese with this book. Studying a foreign language requires active effort. With this book you can be passive and still learn Japanese, as the language is conveniently presented in order of importance.

You can start at anywhere in this book. Skim through and find a word that interests you. Or, if you are a beginner to intermediate Japanese learner, start from #1. When you master these 2000 words and phrases, you will be comfortable with not just living in or visiting Japan, but also attending schools or having a business conversation with a native Japanese speaker.

Ready? Let's get started!

"wa" is a topic marker + "ga" is a subject marker

THE 2000 MOST COMMON WORDS IN JAPANESE

Here are your 2000 Japanese words. As previously stated in the **Introduction,** these are arranged by their frequency of use in both written and spoken Japanese. Feel free to rearrange them during your practice as you encounter the words in your reading, watching or listening to Japanese media, or in conversation with Japanese people.

1- の**/no** [p. case] possessive; *in, at, for, by, of*

これは私の妹の写真です。

This is a picture **of my** little sister.

Kore wa watashi no imōto no shashindesu

2- に**/ni** [p. case] location; **on, in, to, for**

ディズニーランドに行きたいです。

I want to go **to** Disneyland.

Dizunīrando ni ikitai desu

3- は**/wa** [p] topic maker

それは私のではありません。

That **is** not mine.

Sore wa watashi no monode wa arimasen

4- た**/ta** [aux] indicates past tense

今日は仕事に行きました。

I **went** to work today.

Kyō shukkin shimashita

5- を**/o** [p. case] objective, accusative

これを読んでください。

Please read this.

Kore o yonde kudasai

6- だ/da [aux] copula; *be; is*

このゲームは君の勝ちだ。
You **are** the winner in this game.
Kono gēmu hakimi no kasoda

7- が/ga [p. case] nominative, subjective

これが読みたかった本です。
This is the book I wanted to read.
kore wa watashi ga yomitakatta hondesu

8- て/te [p. conj] reason

足が痛くて、歩けない。
My feet hurt **so** I can't walk.
Ashi ga itakute arukenai

9- と/to [p. case] *and, with*

妻とビーチに行きました。
I went to the beach **with** my wife.
Tsuma bichi ni ikimashita

10- ます/masu [aux] indicates respect for the listener

お荷物は明日お届けします。
We will deliver your package tomorrow.
onimotsu ha ashita o todoke shimasu

11- も/mo [p] *too, also*

これも明日までの宿題だ。
This homework is **also** due tomorrow.
kore mo ashita made no shukudai da

12- で/de [p. case] location or time; *in, at, from, by*

あの公園で会いましょう。
Let's meet **at** the park.
ano kōen de aimashō

13- てる/teru [aux] indicates continuing action or state; *be - ing*

赤ちゃんが鳥を見てる。
The baby **is** looking at the bird.
akachan gatori o miteru

9

-11-20

14- ている/te iru [aux, cp] indicates continuing action or state; *be -ing*

ずっと音楽が鳴っている。

The music **is** still play**ing**.

Zutto ongaku ganatte iru

15- です/desu [aux] copula-polite; *be, is*

これが私の家です。

This **is** my house.

kore ga watashi no ie desu

16- れる/reru [aux] indicates passive voice

ふつうに使われる交通機関は電車です。

The transportation normally **used** is the train.

Futsū ni tsuka wareru kō tsūki kan wa den sha desu

17- という/to iu, to yuu [cp] *called, named*

これが、マカロンというお菓子です。

This is a confectionary **called** a macaron.

kore ga makaron to iu okashi desu

18- つう（通）/tsuu [na-adj] *connoisseur, authority*

通な人が好む店だ。

This is a shop that **connoisseurs** are fond of.

tsū na hito ga kono mu mise da

19- こと（事）/koto [n] *thing, matter*

お話ししたい事があります。

I have a **matter** that I would like to talk about.

o wana shishi tai koto gā ri masu

20- ええ/ee [interj] *yes, well*

ええ、私もそう思います。

Yes, I think so too.

ee, watashi mo sō omoimasu

21- えー/ee [interj] *what? eh?*

えー、うそでしょ。

What? Surely, that's a lie!

ee, uso desho

10

22- 言う/iu, yuu [v] *say, speak, talk*

みんなが違う事を言う。

Everyone **says** something different.

minnaga chigau koto o iu

23- あの、あのう、あのー/ano, anoo [interj] *uh, ah, er*

あの、すみませんが、バス停への道を教えてください。

Er, excuse me. Please show me the way to the bus stop.

Ano, sumimasenga, basu tei heno michi o oshie teku dashi

24- まあ/maa [adv] *just*

これでまあいいと思うよ。

I think this is **just** fine.

kore de mā ī to omō yo

25- まー/maa [interj] *Wow! Oh, my goodness!*

まー、すごい！

Wow! That's great!

mā! sugoi

26- ある/aru [v] *be, exist, happen, occur*

土曜日にコンサートがある。

There **is** a concert this Saturday.

do yō hi ni konsā to go aru

27- ね/ne [p. disc] sentence ending; request for agreement or confirmation

このバッグはあなたのですよね。

This is your bag, **isn't it?**

kono baggu wānatano des yo ne

28- ない/nai [aux] negative suffix; *not*

その映画には興味がないです。

I am **not** interested in that movie.

sono eiga niwa kyōmi ganai desu

29- なる/naru [v] intransitive; *become, get, to be, to result in*

大きくなったら、何になる。

What are you going **to be** when you grow up?

ō kiku natta ra nani ni naru

11

1-12-20

30- か/ka [p] sentence ending; indicates a question

この電車はどこに行きますか。

Where does this train go?

kono densho wado koni Ikimasuka

31- その/sono [adj] *that*

その本はもう読みました。

I have already read **that** book.

sono hon wa mō yomi mashita

32- けれど/keredo [conj] *but, however, although*

何度も聞いたけれど、よくわかりません。

I have asked many times, **but** I still don't understand.

Nando mo kitakeredo, yoku wakarimasen

33- から/kara [p. case] *from*

駅から学校まではどのくらいかかりますか。

How long does it take to get to the school **from** the station?

eki kara gakkō made wado no kura Ikakarimasuka

34- よう/yoo [aux] inducement, speculation

お昼ごはんを食べよう。

Let's eat lunch.

o hiru go wano taba yō

35- 思う/omou [v] *think, believe, feel, expect*

それはいいアイディアではないと思う。

I don't **think** that's a good idea.

sore wai ai dei a de wana ito omou

36- 物/mono [n] *thing, object*

重い物は棚の上に置かないでください。

Please do not put heavy **objects** on the shelf.

omoi mono wa tana no ueni o kanai deku dasai

37- そう/soo [adv] *in that way, so, such, that's right*

そうですよね。

Yes, **that's so right**, isn't it?

sō desu yo ne

38- 何/nani, nan [pron] *what, something, anything,*

12

7-13-20

nothing

これは**何**の料理ですか。

What dish is this?

kore wa nanno ryōri desuka

39- 私/watashi [pron] *I, me*

私は日本語の教師です。

I am a Japanese teacher.

watashi wa nihongo no kyōshi desu

40- しまう/shimau [v] transitive; *to finish, to close, end up doing*

この**作業**は早く終わらせて**しまう**ほうがいい。

It is best that we finish **up** this task quickly.

kono sagyō na hayakuo wara sete shimau hō gai

41- それ/sore [p] *that*

それをここに**持**ってきてもらえますか。

Can you please bring **that** here?

sore o koko ni motte kite morae masuka

42- とか/to ka [p conj] *and or, such, like, among other things*

牛乳やバター**とか**は**後**で**買**おう。

Let's get things **like** milk **and** butter later.

gyū nyū yo batta toka wāto de kaō

43- この/kono [adj] *this*

このお店に入りましょう。

Let's go into **this** store.

kono o mise rima shō

44- 無い/nai [i-adj] *not being there*

その**書類**はこのオフィスには**無い**です。

The document **is not** in this office.

sono sho rui wa kono ofuisu ni wa nai desu

45- 行く/iku [v] *go, move, come, proceed*

このプロジェクトがいい**方向**に**行く**といいね。

I hope this project **goes** in the right direction.

Kono purojiekuto gai nōkō ni iku to ī ne

46- んだ/n da [cp] assertive expression; *it is that; the fact is that*

本当のことを言うと、その花瓶は私が壊したんだ。

To tell you the truth, I broke the vase.

hontō no koto iu to sono kabin wa watashi ga kore shi ta nda

47- のだ/no da [cp] assertive expression; *it is that; the fact is that*

この法律は 19世紀に作られた**のだ**。

This law was made in the 19th century.

Kono hōritsu wa 19 seiki ni tsukurareta noda

48- せる/seru [aux] indicates causative or being granted a permission

このゴミは彼に片付けさせるつもりです。

I will **make** him clean up this mess.

Kono gomi wa kare ni kata zu ni sa seru no mori desu

49- これ/kore [pron] *this*

どうぞ、**これ**をお持ちください。

Please take **this** with you.

Dōzo, kore o o mochi kudasai

50- もう/moo [adv] *soon, already, again*

もう夏休みは終わりです。

The summer break is **already** over.

Mō natsuyasumi wa owaridesu

51- である/de aru [cp] copula-formal *be, is*

新消費税率は 10%**である**。

The new consumption tax rate **is** 10%.

Atarashī shōhizei-ritsu wa 10-pāsentode aru

52- 時/toki [n] *time, hour, occasion*

景気のいい**時**は、よく物が売れる。

Goods sell well **when** the economy is good.

keiki no ī toki wa, yoku mono ga ureru

53- な/na [p. disc] sentence ending; indicates emphasized

14

emotion

この映画はつまらない**な**。

This movie is so boring!

Kono eiga wa tsumarani na

54- ず/zu [aux] **not doing**

文句を言わ**ず**にいられない。

I cannot stand by **without complaining**.

Monku o irezu ni rarenai

55- ので/node [p. conj] *because, since, because of*

値段が高かった**ので**、買うのをやめた。

I did not buy it **because** it was expensive.

Nedan ga takakattanode, kau no o yameta

56- んで/n de [p. conj] *because, since, because of*

金曜日はレストランが混む**んで**、土曜日に行こう。

Since the restaurant will be crowded on Friday, let's go on Saturday.

Kin'yōbi wa resutoran ga komu n de, doyōbi ni ikai

57- 人/hito [n] *person, people, human being*

世界には多くの**人**がいます。

There are a lot of **people** in the world.

Sekai ni wa ōku no hito ga imasu

58- よ/yo [p. disc] sentence ending; indicates certainty, emphasis, request

急いだほうがいい**よ**。

We'd better hurry up!

Isoida hō ga ī yo

59- こう/koo [adv] *so, like this, in this way*

その算数の問題は**こう**すると解けるよ。

The math problem can be solved **like this**.

Sono sansū no mondai wa kō suruto tokeru yo

60- ば/ba [p. conj] *if...then, when*

このプロジェクトが終われ**ば**、休みが取れます。

When this project is over, I can go on a vacation.

Kono purojekuto ga owareba, kasumi ga toremasu

61- や/ya [p] *such things as, ... and/or ...*

赤や黄色の花が咲いている。

Red **and** yellow flowers are in bloom.

Aka ya-jō-iro no hana ga saite iru

62- 来る/kuru [v] *come*

もうすぐ春が来る。

Spring **is coming** soon.

Mōsugu harugakuru

63- まで（迄）/made [p] *to, till, until*

シフトは5時までです。

My shift is **till** 5 o'clock.

Shifuto wa 5-jimadedesu

64- 見る/miru [v] *see, look, watch, check*

よく見ると、小さな穴があるね。

If you **look** closely, there is a small hole.

Yokumiruto, chisana ana aru ne

65- たり/tari [p] *-ing and -ing (representative)*

歌ったり、踊ったりするのが好きです。

I like doing things like sing**ing and** danc**ing**.

utatsu tari, odoritsu tari suru no ga sukidesu

66- 今/ima [n] *now*

今はまだお腹が空いていない。

I am not hungry **now**.

ima wa mada onaka ga suite inai

67- 良い/yoi, ii [i-adj] *good, nice, fine*

この前の試験で良い成績をとりました。

I got a **good** score on the recent exam.

konomae no shiken de yoi seiseki o torimashita

68- いい/ii [i-adj] *good, nice, fine*

いいレストランを知っています。

I know a **nice** restaurant.

T restutoran o chitsute imasu

16

生きがい - reason to live / purpose
(ikigai)

69- 所/tokoro [n] place, point, site, part, aspect

住むのに一番便利な所はどこですか。

Where is the most convenient **place** to live?

Sumu no ni-ban benrina tokoro wa dokodesu ka

70- 自分/jibun [pron] myself, yourself, oneself, I, me

自分の問題は自分で解決しなさい。

Solve **your own** problems **yourself**.

Jibun no mondai wa jibun de kaiketsu shi nasai

71- ん一/nn [interj] uh, huh, hmm, yeah

ん一、よくわかりません。

Hmm, I am not so sure.

N-, yoku wakarimasen

72- あ一/aa [interj] er, uh, um, Ah! Oh!

あ一、危ない！

Ah, watch out!

A-, abunai

73- やはり/yahari [adv] too, also, still, even so, as expected

やはり、私も同じ気持ちです。

There you have it, still, I am of that train of thought **too**.

Yahari watashi mo onaji kimochidesu

74- やっぱり/yappari [adv] too, also, still, even so, as expected

やっぱり、あなたが思った通りになりましたね。

Ultimately, it turned out just **as you expected**.

Yappari, anata ga omotta tōri ni narimashita ne

75- たい/tai [aux] want to ..., would like to ...

私も一緒に行きたいです。

I **want to** go with you.

watashi mo- issha ni ikitai desu

76- やる/yaru [v] transitive do, undertake, make, give

そのゲームをやると楽しいでしょうね。

It would be fun to **play** that game.

Sono gēmu o yaru to tanoshideshou ne

77- 中/naka [n] *inside, in, into*

早く家の中に入りなさい。

Come **inside** the house quickly!

Hayaku ie naka ni hairi nasai

78- いる/iru [v] *be, exist, stay*

ドアの向こうにいるのは誰。

Who **is** behind the door?

Doa no mukō ni iru no wa dare

79- 出来る/dekiru [v] *be able to, be ready*

テニスが出来るようになるためには練習が必要だ。

Practice is necessary to **be able to** play tennis.

Tenisu ga dekiru yō ni naru tame ni wa renshū ga hitsuyōda.

80- など/nado [p] *et cetera, or something, and so on*

そのお店には食器や家具などがあります。

That store has tableware, furniture, **and so on.**

Sono o-ten ni hashokki ya nado ga arimasu

81- として/toshite [cp] *as, for*

私は親として責任があります。

I am responsible **as a parent.**

Watashi wa oya to shite sekinin ga arimasu

82- 後/ato [n] *behind, after, later*

この後、日本語のレッスンに行きます。

After this, I will go to a Japanese lesson.

Kono ato, nihongo no ressun ni ikimasu

83- また/mata [adv] *again, and, also, still*

また会いましょう。

See you **again.**

Mata aimashou

84- ちょっと/chotto [adv] *just a little, a bit*

ちょっと話しましょう。

Let's have **a little** talk.

Chotto hanashimashou

18

85- てくる/te kuru [cp] *do and come back*

買い物に行ってくる。

I'm **going** shopping.

86- だけ/dake [p] *only, alone, merely, just*

自分の荷物だけ持ってください。

Please hold **only** your own luggage.

87- くらい/kurai [p] *about, around, approximately, at least, to the extent*

おこずかいは五千円くらいほしい。

I want **about** five thousand yen for pocket money.

88- ぐらい/gurai [p] *about, around, approximately, at least, to the extent*

自分の弁当ぐらいは自分で作らないといけない。

You should **at least** prepare your own lunch.

89- ではない/de wa nai [cp] *is/am/are not, it is not the case that ...*

私は店員ではない。

I **am not** a staff member.

90- えーと/eto [interj] *let me see, well, errr*

えーと、今度の母の日のプレゼントは何にしようかな。

Well, what present should I get for Mother's Day?

91- 方/hoo [n] *direction, way, side, method*

こっちの方にきてください。

Please come this **way**.

92- ていく/te iku [cp] *indicates direction toward a location*

歩いて**いく**ならスニーカーを履きましょう。

If we're going to walk **there**, let's wear sneakers.

93- てく/te ku [cp] *indicates direction toward a location*

明日はどのバッグを持っ**てく**の。

Which bag are you going to take **there** tomorrow?

94- 訳/wake [n] *reason, cause*

けんかになった**訳**は何なの。

What was the **reason** for the fight?

95- へ/e [p. case] destination; *to, towards*

先生**へ**手紙を書こう。

Write a letter **to** the teacher.

96- どう/doo [adv] *how, in what way*

このお店は**どう**ですか。

How about this store?

97- し/shi [p. conj] *indicates more than one reason*

わたしは宿題もやった**し**、庭の掃除もした。

I did my homework **and** cleaned the garden.

98- 本当/hontoo [n] *truth, real, right*

その話は**本当**ですか。

Is the story **true**?

99- 持つ/motsu [v] *have, hold, carry, possess*

私はいつも右手でペンを**持つ**。

I always **hold** my pen in my right hand.

100- 出る/deru [v] *go out, come out, leave, exit, attend*

午前中にホテルを出る。

I will **leave** the hotel in the morning.

101- 為/tame [n] *for, benefit, sake*

私は健康の為に野菜を食べます。

I eat vegetables **for** my health.

102- すごい/sugoi [i-adj] *fantastic, wonderful, amazing*

サーカスのアクロバットはすごい！

The circus acrobatics are **amazing**!

103- 考える/kangaeru [v] *think about, take into consideration*

自分の未来について考える。

I **think about** my future.

104- そこ/soko [n] *there, then*

そこの看板には何と書いてありますか。

What is written on the signboard **there**?

105- う/u [aux] *solicitation*

映画を観に行こう。

Let's go see a movie.

106- 分かる/wakaru [v] *understand, see, become clear*

あなたの気持ちは分かる。

I **understand** your feelings.

107- ておる/te oru* [cp] continuation polite; *be ...ing, have been ...ing*

私は子供に柔道を教えております。

I **am** teach**ing** judo to children.

*The phrase "te oru" is almost always used in its extended polite form of "te orimasu".

108- について/ni tsuite [cp] *about, concerning, with regard to*

日本の歴史について知りたいです。

I want to learn **about** Japanese history.

109- それで/sore de [conj] *and then, so, because of that, upon*

この町は子供が多い。それで児童館が作られました。

This town has many children. **Because of that**, they opened a children's center.

110- 入る/hairu [v] *enter, come in, go into*

東の入り口からビルに入る。

Enter the building from the east entrance.

111- 作る/tsukuru [v] *make, create, produce, build*

学校で宇宙基地の模型を作る。

We **make** a model of a space base at school.

112- てみる/te miru [cp] *try to do something*

新しいレシピでカレーを作ってみる。

I am going to **try** making curry with a new recipe.

113- 聴く/kiku [v] *hear, listen to*

車でラジオを聴く。

I **listen to** the radio in the car.

22

114- 聞く/kiku [v] *hear, ask*

駅で行き先を聞く。

I will **ask for** directions at the station.

115- そして/soshite [conj] *and, so, and then*

私は留学をしました。そして外交官になりました。

I studied abroad, **and then** became a diplomat.

116- くれる/kureru [v] *to let one have, to be given*

このストーリータイムはぬり絵をくれる。

You will **be given** a coloring sheet at this story time.

117- 場合/baai [n] *case, situation*

咳がでる場合はマスクをしてください。

In case you have a cough, please wear a mask.

118- 話/hanashi [n] *talk, story*

彼からおもしろい話を聞いた。

I heard an interesting **story** from him.

119- ながら/nagara [p. conj] *with, over, while, during*

車を運転しながら携帯を見てはいけない。

You mustn't use a cell phone **while** driving.

120- そんな/sonna [adj] *such, that*

私はそんなケースを聞いたことがない。

I have never heard of **such** a case.

121- 使う/tukau [v] *use, handle*

今日は新しいカードを使う。

I am **using** a new card today.

23

122- 日本/nihon, nippon [n] *Japan*

日本は島国です。

Japan is an island nation.

123- 風/fuu [na-adj] *style, way, manner*

これは関東風のうどんです。

This is Kanto **style** udon.

124- おー/oo [interj] *Oh!, Wow!*

おー、一番だ！

Wow, I came first!

125- 前/mae [n] *front, ago, before*

家の前に車をとめる。

Park your car in **front** of the house.

126- 多い/ooi [i-adj] *many, much*

このタワーマンションは独身の人が多い。

This apartment tower has **many** single people.

127- よく/yoku [adv] *nicely, well, frequently*

このレポートはとてもよく書かれている。

This report is **well** written.

128- 一つ、ひとつ/hito-tsu [num] *one (piece, thing)*

そのケーキを一つください。

Please give me **one** piece of cake.

129- 子供/kodomo [n] *child(ren)*

子供部屋のある家を探しています。

We are looking for a house with a **children**'s room.

130- 非常/hijoo [na-adj] *emergency, extremely, extraordinary*

非常の時は 119番してください。

Please call 119 in the event of an **emergency**.

131- 気/ki [n] *spirit, mind, heart, intention, feeling*

やる気になれば何でもできる。

You can do anything if you set your **mind** to it.

132- ても/te mo [p. conj] *even if, even though, no matter how ...*

いくら注意しても、彼は同じ間違いをする。

He makes the same mistakes **no matter how** careful he tries to be.

133- 取る/toru [v] *take, get*

テストで満点を取る。

Get a perfect score on the test.

134- うち/uchi [n] *inside*

箱のうちがわに説明があります。

There is an explanation on the **inside** the box.

135- 知る/shiru [v] *know, be aware of*

インターネットで地震についてのニュースを知った。

I **became aware of** news about an earthquake from the Internet.

136- より/yori [p. case] *than, from*

私は猫より犬が好きだ。

I like dogs more **than** cats.

137- それから/sore kara [conj] *and then*

夕食を食べて、それから風呂に入りました。

I had dinner, **and then** took a bath.

138- うー/uu [interj] *Woo!, Aww! Ugh!*

うー、困ったな！

Aww, I'm in trouble.

139- 感じ/kanji [n] *feeling, impression, atmosphere*

あまり**感じ**のいい店員ではなかった。

The store clerk did not leave a very good **impression**.

140- みたい/mitai [na-adj] *like, sort of, similar to*

ビーチで子供**みたい**に遊ぶ。

Play **like** a kid when you're at the beach.

141- でも/demo [conj] *but, though*

私たちのチームはよく戦いました。**でも**、ゲームに勝つことはできませんでした。

Our team fought so hard, **but** we could not win the game.

142- ここ/koko [pron] *here*

ここにあった本がどこにあるか知りませんか。

Do you know what happened to the book that was **here**?

143- とっても/tottemo [adv] *very, awfully, extremely*

私はこのくまのキャラクターが**とっても**好きです。

I like this bear character **very** much.

144- とても/totemo [adv] *very, awfully, extremely*

今日は**とても**大きな犬を連れている人に会った。

I met a man with an **extremely** big dog today.

145- いろいろ/iroiro [na-adj] *various*

この本屋は**いろいろな**ジャンルの本を売っている。

This bookstore sells **various** genres of books.

146- 一/ichi [num] *one*

一から順に数える。

Count in order from **one**.

147- 一番/ichiban [n] [adv] *number one, first, most*

一番高い携帯電話はどれですか。

Which is **the most** expensive cell phone?

148- 二/ni [num] *two*

ねこを二匹飼っています。

I have **two** cats.

149- 同じ/onaji [adn] *same*

この前と同じ場所で会いましょう。

See you at the **same** place as the last time.

150- まず/mazu [adv] *first of all, to start with, first*

まず、あなたの親切さに感謝したいと思います。

First, I would like to thank you for your kindness.

151- 必要/hitsuyoo [na-adj] [n] *necessary, necessity*

パスポートの更新に必要な書類を用意する。

Prepare the **necessary** documents for renewing your passport.

152- 仕事/shigoto [n] *work, job, occupation, task*

今日は仕事があります。

I have **work** to do today.

153- 余り、あまり/amari [adv] [n] *not very, remainder*

反応はあまり良くありませんでした。

The response was **not very** favorable.

154- によって/ni yotte [cp] *by, according to, due to, because of, depending on*

台風によって、イベントは中止になりました。

The event was canceled **due to** the typhoon.

155- かもしれない/ka mo shire nai [cp] *may, perhaps, possibly*

住所を間違ったかもしれない。

You **may** have gotten the address wrong.

156- 僕/boku [pron] *I, me (male/boy term)*

僕のサッカーのシューズはどこ。

Where are **my** soccer shoes?

157- 皆, みんな/minna [n] *all, everyone, everybody, everything*

みんなの意見を聞いてプランを決めよう。

Listen to **everyone**'s opinions and decide on a plan.

158- 彼/kare [pron] *he him, boyfriend*

彼は私の中学校の同級生だ。

He is my junior high school classmate.

159- 食べる/taberu [v] *eat*

午前7時に朝食を食べる。

I **eat** breakfast at 7:00 AM.

160- ほど/hodo [p] indicates approx. amount or maximum limit

私の親ほど心配性のある人はいない。

No one worries **as much as** my parents do.

161-しかし/shikashi [conj] *however, but*

けんかは終わりました。**しかし**、仲良しになったとはいえない。

The fight is over. **However**, you couldn't say that they have become friends.

162- 書く/kaku [v] *write, compose*

私は毎日日記を**書く**。

I **write** a diary every day.

163- 入れる/ireru [v] *put in, insert*

食料品をかごに**入れる**。

Put your groceries **in** the basket.

164- 次/tsugi [n] *next*

次は東京駅です。

The **next** stop is Tokyo Station.

165- 結構/kekkoo [na-adj] *nice, fine, quite*

料理がとても**結構**なお味だった。

The food was quite delicious.

166- 問題/mondai [n] *problem, question*

算数の**問題**が難しい。

The math **question** is difficult.

167- 例えば/tatoeba [adv] *for example, such as*

例えば生まれかわるなら何になりたいですか。

For example, what would you like to be reborn as?

168- 目/me [n] *eye, eyeball*

赤ちゃんの目はかわいい。

Babies' **eyes** are adorable.

169- 眼/me [n] *eye, eyeball*

眼が悪くなったのでめがねがいる。

My **eyes** are getting worse, so I will need glasses.

170- 頃/goro [n] *time, around, about*

四月頃にはさくらが咲くだろう。

The cherry blossoms will bloom **around** April.

171- 上/ue [n] *above, up, over, top*

これは上からの指示だ。

These instructions are from the **top**.

172- くださる/kudasaru [v] *to give, to bestow, to kindly do for one*

お隣の方はよくお菓子をくださる。

The neighbors often **give** me treats.

173- 他/hoka [n] *other, the rest, outside, beyond*

これの他にほしいものはない。

There is nothing that I want **other** than this.

174- いつ/itsu [adv] *when, how soon*

お父さんはいつ帰ってくるの。

When will my dad come home?

175- 家/ie [n] *house, family, household, home*

家の電話に連絡をください。
Please contact me at my **home** phone number.

176- 日/hi [n] *day, days*

今日はパーティに行く日だ。
Today is the **day** to go to the party.

177- 付く/tsuku [v] *to be attached, to stick, to accompany*

お子様セットにはおもちゃが付く。
The kid's meal **comes with** a toy.

178- 出す/dasu [v] *to take out, to put out*

火曜日はリサイクルのゴミを出す日だ。
Tuesday is the day to **put out** recycling garbage.

179- 一人/hitori [n] *one person, along, solitary*

子供は一人しかいません。
There is only **one** child.

180- 人間/ningen [n] *human being, person, man, character*

猿と人間の違いはなんだろう。
What is the difference between monkeys and **humans**?

181- どこ/doko [pron] *where, what place*

この迷子の親はどこだろう。
Where are this lost child's parents?

182- 時間/jikan [n] *time, hours*

時間を忘れて暗くなるまで遊んでしまった
I forgot about the **time** and played until it was dark.

183- ただ/tada [adj] *ordinary, common*

これは**ただ**のおもちゃの汽車です。

This is an **ordinary** toy train.

184- だから/dakara [conj] *so, therefore*

今日はデートがある。**だから**、早く帰りたいんだ。

I have a date today. **So**, I want to go home early.

185- 違う/chigau [v] *to differ, to vary*

僕らの意見はいつも**違う**。

Our opinions are always **different**.

186- 受ける/ukeru [v] *receive, get, catch*

サッカーのゴールキーパーがシュートを**受ける**。

In soccer, the goalkeeper tries to **catch** the shot.

187- 言葉/kotoba [n] *language, dialect, words, phrase, remark*

大事なことを伝えるには、**言葉**は選んだ方がいい。

You should choose your **words** carefully when you talk about matters of importance.

188- なんか/nanka [p] *things like, or something like that*

彼女の誕生日プレゼントにこのネックレス**なんか**どうですか。

How about **something like** this necklace for her birthday present？

189- 少し/sukoshi [adv] *small, a little*

少し寒くなってきたようだ。

It seems to be getting **a little** cold.

190- まま/mama [p] *as it is*

その**まま**にしておいてください。

Please leave it **as it is**.

191- 買う/kau [v] *buy, purchase*

コンビニでお弁当を買う。

I **buy** lunch at a convenience store.

192- まだ/mada [adv] *as yet, still*

まだ夏休みの宿題がいっぱい残っている。

I **still** have a lot of summer homework.

193- 手/te [n] *hand, arm*

手遊びのグーチョキパー知っている？

Do you know about the **hand** game, Rock Paper Scissors?

194- 話す/hanasu [v] *talk, speak*

赤ちゃんは何ヶ月から話すようになるのだろう。

I wonder at how many months the baby will start **speaking**.

195- 好き/suki [v] *like, love*

私は古い映画が好きです。

I **like** old movies.

196- 返る/kaeru [v] *return, come back*

落とし物が持ち主に返る。

Lost items may **return** to their owners.

197- てもらう/temorau [cp] *to have someone do something*

お父さんにこのおもちゃを買ってもらう。

I will **have** my father **buy** this toy.

198- 掛ける/kakeru [v] *to hang*

上着をハンガーに掛けてください。

Hang your jacket on a hanger, please.

199- 終わる/owaru [v] *to finish, to end*

もう少しでこのプロジェクトが**終わる**。

This project will be **finished** soon.

200- 意味/imi [n] *meaning, sense*

上司の言っている言葉の**意味**がわからない。

I don't understand what my boss **means**.

201- のである/no de aru [cp] *assertion*

この公園はオリンピックを記念してつくられた**のである**。

This park was built to commemorate the Olympics.

202- いろんな/ironna [adn] *various*

この絵は**いろんな**色が使われているね。

This picture uses **various** colors.

203- 付ける/tsukeru [v] *put, attach, apply*

虫刺されにかゆみ止めを**付ける**。

Apply anti-itch cream on insect bites.

204- 形/katachi [n] *form, shape, figure*

まる、三角、四角の他にどんな形があるだろう。

What other **shapes** are there besides circles, triangles and squares?

205- かなり/kanari [adv] *considerably, quite*

今度の台風は**かなり**大きいらしい。

The next typhoon seems to be **quite** big.

206- 三/san [num] *three*

一、二、三の合図で鬼ごっこしよう。

Let's play tag on the count of one, two, and **three**.

207- 最初/saisho [n] *first*

最初は誰でもわからない事が多い。

There are many things that no one understands at **first**.

208- 間/aida [n] *distance, period, between*

この壁と壁の間に棚を作ります。

We will build a shelf **between** these walls.

209- 感じる/kanjiru [v] *feel*

今朝の風は肌に寒く感じる。

This morning's wind **feels** cold on my skin.

210- しか/shika [p] *only, just, no more than*

財布に百円しか入っていない。

I **only** have one-hundred yen in my wallet.

211- かかる/kakaru [v] *hang, take, cost*

この家を改築するにはかなりの費用がかかる。

It will **cost** a lot to renovate this house.

212- 大きな/ookina [adj] *big, great*

人間の子供ぐらいの大きな犬がいた。

There was a **big** dog about the size of a human child.

213- 住む/sumu [v] *live*

このアパートに住むことにしよう。

We will **live** in this apartment.

214- 最近/saikin [adj] *recently, lately*

最近は高齢者による車の事故が増えている。

Recently, car accidents caused by elderly people are increasing.

215- 特に/tokuni [adv] *especially, particularly*

最近は特に STEM コースに人気がある。

STEM courses have been **particularly** popular lately.

216- 誰/dare [pron] *whom whose, whom*

ここに荷物を置いたのは誰ですか。

Who left their luggage here?

217- こんな/konna [adn] *such, like that*

こんなおいしいケーキは食べたことがない。

I have never eaten **such** a delicious cake.

218- 友達/tomodachi [n] *friend*

友達は一生の宝だ。

Friends are a lifetime treasure.

219- 大きい/ookii [i-adj] *big, great, large*

あそこに見える大きい家が祖父の家です。

The **large** house over there is my grandfather's.

220- すぐ/sugu [adv] *soon*

この書類をすぐに届けてもらえますか。

Can you deliver this document **soon**?

221- 一緒/issho [n] *together, with*

友達と一緒にディナーに行った。

I went out for dinner **with** a friend.

222- 生活/seekatsu [n] *life*

<ruby>新<rt>あたら</rt></ruby>しい<ruby>街<rt>まち</rt></ruby>での<ruby>生活<rt>せいかつ</rt></ruby>はどうですか。
How's **life** in the new city?

223- 国/kuni [n] *country*

<ruby>違<rt>ちが</rt></ruby>う<ruby>国<rt>くに</rt></ruby>から<ruby>来<rt>き</rt></ruby>た<ruby>人<rt>ひと</rt></ruby>と<ruby>友達<rt>ともだち</rt></ruby>になった。
I became friends with people who came from different **countries**.

224- あげる/ageru [v] *raise, lift*

<ruby>質問<rt>しつもん</rt></ruby>がある<ruby>人<rt>ひと</rt></ruby>は、<ruby>手<rt>て</rt></ruby>をあげてください。
If you have any questions, please **raise** your hand.

225- あんた/anta [pron] *you (informal)*

あんたは<ruby>最近<rt>さいきん</rt></ruby>どうしてるの。
How have **you** been lately?

226- あなた/anata [pron] *you*

あなたの<ruby>今日<rt>きょう</rt></ruby>の<ruby>予定<rt>よてい</rt></ruby>は<ruby>何<rt>なん</rt></ruby>ですか。
What is **your** plan for today?

227- 現在/genzai [n] *current, now*

<ruby>現在<rt>げんざい</rt></ruby>の<ruby>気温<rt>きおん</rt></ruby>は<ruby>二十六度<rt>にじゅうろくど</rt></ruby>です。
The **current** temperature is 26 degrees.

228- 高い/takai [i-adj] *high, tall, expensive*

<ruby>日本<rt>にほん</rt></ruby>ではバターの<ruby>値段<rt>ねだん</rt></ruby>が<ruby>高<rt>たか</rt></ruby>いね。
Butter is **expensive** in Japan.

229- なんて/nante [adv] *how ...! what...!*

なんて<ruby>親切<rt>しんせつ</rt></ruby>な<ruby>人<rt>ひと</rt></ruby>だろう。
How kind he is!

230- 悪い/warui [i-adj] *bad*

悪いのは僕だ。

It was my **bad**.

231- 気持ち/kimochi [n] *feeling*

彼女の気持ちを傷つけたくない。

I don't want to hurt her **feelings**.

232- 乗る /noru [v] *ride, get on, take*

ジェットコースターは一番後ろに乗るのが好きだ。

I like **riding** at the back of rollercoasters.

233- において/ni oi te [cp] *at, in, on*

音楽において、彼の才能は特別だ。

He is exceptionally talented **in** music.

234- 見える/mieru [v] *can see, be seen*

ビルの高層階から見える眺めは最高だ。

The view I **can see** from the high floors of the building is amazing.

235- 変わる/kawaru [v] *change, transform*

水は温度によって質が変わる。

Water's state **changes** with its temperature.

236- べし/beshi [aux] *must, should*

お寺では靴は脱ぐべしと注意書きがある。

At the temple, there is a notice saying that we **should** remove our shoes.

237- あるいは/aruiwa [conj] *or, perhaps*

ランチ、あるいはお茶をしましょう。

Let's get together for lunch **or** tea.

238- 大変/taihen [na-adj] *serious, terrible, difficult*

大変な問題がおきた。

A **serious** problem occurred.

239- による/ni yoru [cp] *due to, based on*

性別による差別は禁止されている。

Discrimination **based on** gender is prohibited.

240- 会社/kaisha [n] *company, firm*

会社の電話番号が新しくなった。

The **company** got a new phone number.

241- ほとんど/hotondo [adv] *most, almost, nearly*

ほとんどの人は電車で仕事に行く。

Most people take a train to go to work.

242- 実際/jissai [n] *actually, in fact*

実際、魚料理は好きではない。

In fact, I don't like fish dishes.

243- 先生/sensee [n] *teacher*

空手の先生から礼儀を教わった。

I learned manners from my karate **teacher**.

244- 彼女/kanojo [pron] *she, girlfriend*

今週末は彼女とデートする。

I have a date with my **girlfriend** this weekend.

245- 二人/futari [n] *two people, a couple*

このゴンドラは二人乗りだ。

This gondola is for **two people**.

246- 心/kokoro [n] *mind, heart*

心から感謝する。

I thank you from the bottom of my **heart**.

247- らしい/rashii [aux] *seem, look*

この道の先で事故があったらしい。

It **seems** there has been an accident down the road.

248- 金/kane [n] *money*

金のなる木が欲しい。

I wish I had a **money** tree.

249- 顔/kao [n] *face*

このタオルで顔を拭いてください。

Please wipe your **face** with this towel.

250- いただく/itadaku [v] *to receive (humble)*

昔の先生から贈り物をいただく。

I sometimes **receive** gifts from my old teacher.

251- ずっと/zutto [adv] *all the time, for a long time*

ずっと秘密にしていることがある。

I have a secret that I have been keeping **for a long time**.

252- さらに/sarani [adv] *moreover, further, additionally*

さらに最新の治療法が研究されている。

New treatments are being researched **further**.

253- 町/machi [n] *town, city*

この町には小学校が二つある。

There are two elementary schools in this **town**.

254- 街/machi [n] *town, city*

この街は若者に人気のスポットが多い。

This **town** has a lot of spots appealing to young people.

255- 及び/oyobi [conj] *as well as, and*

お年寄り及び子供連れの家族は、先に入場してください。

Elderly people **as well as** families with small children are invited to enter first.

256- 沢山/takusan [adv] *many, much, a lot*

今年のハロウィーンは沢山の人で道が賑わった。

The streets were crowded with **many** people for Halloween this year.

257- いい/ii [adj] *good, fine*

この香水はいい香りがする。

This perfume has a **good** fragrance.

258- 大体/daitai [adv] *approximately, about, almost*

予想値は大体合っていた。

The estimate was **about** accurate.

259- もちろん/mochiron [adv] *of course, needless to say*

もちろん喜んで参加します。

Of course, I will be happy to participate.

260- 読む/yomu [v] *read*

まず教科書を読む。

I **read** my textbook first.

261- 人たち/hito-tachi [n] *people*

パーティでおもしろい人たちに会った。

I met interesting **people** at the party.

262- 今日/kyoo [n] *today*

今日から新学期が始まる。

The new semester starts **today**.

263- 昔/mukashi [n] *ancient times, in the past, long ago*

昔、人々は川で洗濯をしていた。

Long ago, people used to wash clothes in the river.

264-うん／un [interj] *yeah*

「うん」ではなくて、「はい」と返事をしなさい。
When you reply, say "yes' instead of "**yeah**".

265- すべて／subete [n] *everything, all*

時間通りに**すべて**の仕事を終わらせた。
I finished **all** the work on time.

266- 教える／oshieru [v] *teach, tell*

今年から新しい学校で**教える**ことになった。
I am going to **teach** at a new school from this year.

267- 子／ko [n] *child, children*

公園の砂場で小さい**子**が遊んでいる。
Small **children** are playing in the sandpit in the playground.

268- ておく／te oku [cp] *having it done in advance*

この仕事は先に**しておく**ように。
You should **get** this job **done** first.

269- に対して／ni taishite [cp] *towards, regarding*

フォーラムで環境問題**に対して**意見を述べる。
I will be presenting my opinion **regarding** environmental issues at
the forum.

270- ばかり／bakari [p] *only, nothing but*

息子がゲーム**ばかり**している。
My son does **nothing but** play video games.

271- なぜ／naze [adv] *why, how come*

四歳の子供は、いつも「**なぜ**」と言う。
Four-year-olds are always asking "**why**".

272- 水/mizu [n] *water*

運動の前には沢山水を飲んだ方がいい。

You should drink a lot of **water** before exercising.

273- 当時/tooji [n] *then, at that time*

当時はこのあたりは野原だった。

Back **then**, this area was all green fields.

274- 場所/basho[n] *place, spot*

間違えて違う場所に行ってしまった。

I made a mistake and went to a wrong **place**.

275- 置く/oku [v] *put, place, leave behind*

手荷物を席の上の棚に置く。

Put your carry-on bags on the shelf above you.

276- 楽しい/tanoshii [i-adj] *pleasant, happy, enjoyable*

楽しい話が聞けて嬉しい。

I am glad that I got to hear **pleasant** news.

277- にとって/ni totte [cp] *for*

子供にとって、母親の愛情が大切だ。

A mother's love is important **for** children.

278- 声/koe [n] *voice*

声の大きい人がいる。

There is someone with a loud **voice**.

279- 普通/futsuu [na-adj] *ordinary, normal*

普通の人生も悪くない。

Having an **ordinary** life isn't too bad.

280- 残る/nokoru [v] *remain, be left*

十から三を引くと、七が残る。

Ten minus three **leaves** seven.

281- 最後/saigo [n] *last, end*

今日の最後の電車に乗り遅れたら大変だ。

I will be in trouble if I miss the **last** train of the day.

282- 車/kuruma [n] *car, wheel*

地方では買い物に行くのに車がいる。

You need a **car** to go grocery shopping in the countryside.

283- 初めて/hajimete [adv] *first, for the first time*

初めて学校に行く日は緊張した。

I was nervous on my **first** day at school.

284- 今度/kondo [n] *next time*

今度は歌舞伎を観に行きましょう。

Let's go see a Kabuki show **next time**.

285- 体/karada [n] *body*

シャワーで体を洗いなさい。

Wash your **body** in the shower.

286- 私達/watashi-tachi [pron] *we*

私達は新しい所へ引っ越します。

We are moving to a new place.

287- 強い/tsuyoi [i-adj] *strong, powerful*

今年のチームは強い。

Our team is **strong** this year.

288- 全く/mattaku [adv] *entirely, completely, absolutely*

その問題には**全く**気付かなかった。

I was **completely** unaware of the problem.

289- 呼ぶ/yobu [v] *call*

お母さんの**呼ぶ**声が聞こえる。

I hear my mother **calling** out for me.

290- 結局/kekkyoku [adv] *after all, finally*

結局、元の場所に戻ってしまった。

After all, I found myself back at the start.

291- 歩く/aruku [v] *walk*

道を**歩く**時は車に気をつけてください。

Beware of cars when you **walk** on the sidewalk.

292- 男/otoko [n] *man, male*

男の人のトイレはあちらです。

The **men**'s bathroom is over there.

293- 女性/josei [n] *female, woman*

女性向けのシャンプーはいい香りがする。

Women's shampoo has a good fragrance.

294- 学校/gakkoo [n] *school, academy*

学校で学級委員に選ばれた。

I was elected as the class president at **school**.

295- 生きる/ikiru [v] *live*

外国で**生きる**のは大変だ。

It's hard to **live** in a foreign country.

296- なかなか/nakanaka [adv] *fairly, quite*

バイオリンを弾くのが**なかなか**上手にならない。
I can't **quite** make any improvement at playing the violin.

297- 先/saki [n] *prior, end*

漢字よりも**先**にひらがなを学びましょう。
Learn hiragana **prior** to kanji.

298- もっと/motto [adv] *more*

もっと大きな声で返事をするように。
Please answer **louder**.

299- ことが出来る/koto ga dekiru [cp] *can do, be able to*

彼はバイオリンを弾く**ことが出来る**。
He **can** play the violin.

300- テーマ/teema [n] *theme*

この映画の**テーマ**は人権問題だ。
The **theme** of this film is human rights issues.

301- 世界/sekai [n] *the world, society*

世界にはいろいろな食べ物がある。
There are various foods in the **world**.

302- 状態/jootai [n] *state, condition*

今の国際関係は戦前の**状態**に似ている。
The world looks like it's in a pre-war **state** now.

303- もし/moshi [adv] *if, in case*

もし地震が来たら、急いで逃げるように。
If an earthquake strikes, evacuate immediately.

304- 全然/zenzen [adv] *not at all, entirely*

全然痩せないのはなぜだろう。

Why can't you lose weight **at all**?

305- 飲む/nomu [v] *drink, swallow*

運動の前に水を飲む。

Drink water before a workout.

306- 新しい/atarashii [i-adj] *new, fresh*

新しい先生に会うのが楽しみだ。

I'm looking forward to meeting my **new** teacher.

307- はやい/hayai [i-adj] *fast, quick, early*

明日の朝ははやいので今夜はもう寝よう。

Let's go to bed, as we have an **early** start tomorrow morning.

308- 会う/au [v] *meet, encounter, see*

姪っ子が会うたびに大きくなっている。

Every time I **see** my niece, she is getting bigger and bigger.

309- アメリカ/amerika [n] *America, USA, the U.S*

アメリカの西海岸のビーチが好きだ。

I like beaches on the West Coast in **the U.S.**

310- あれ/are [n] *that, something*

あれは何だろう？。

What is **that**?

311- 小さい/chiisai [i-adj] *small, tiny*

小さい貝殻を浜辺でみつけた。

I found **small** seashells on the beach.

312- 相手/aite [n] *companion, partner, other party, opponent*

ネットゲームの相手を募集する。

I am looking for an online game **partner**.

313- 母/haha [n] *one's mother*

母は九州で育ちました。

My mother grew up in Kyushu.

314- 以上/ijoo [n] *not less than, beyond*

この乗り物は五歳以上向けです。

This ride is for children aged 5 years **and older**.

315- 関係/kankei [n] *relation, relationship*

職場でよくある問題は人間関係だ。

One of the most common issues at work is personal **relationships**.

316- 四/yon [num] *four*

ねこを四匹飼っています。

I have **four** cats.

317- たぶん/tabun [adv] *perhaps, probably*

この計算でたぶん合っていると思います。

I think this calculation is **probably** correct.

318- 店/mise [n] *store, resaurant*

食料品のお店に行きたい。

I want to go to a grocery **store**.

319- どんな/ donna [adn] *what kind of*

どんな絵が好きですか。

What kind of art do you like?

320- 頭/atama [n] *head*

自転車に乗る時は、ヘルメットをかぶって頭を守る。
Put on a helmet to protect your **head** when you ride your bicycle.

321- 電話/denwa [n] *(telephone) call, telephone (devise)*

もうすぐ電話がかかってくる時間だ。
I am expecting a **call** soon.

322- 長い/nagai [i-adj] *long (distance, time, length)*

長い夏休みの後は朝起きるのが大変だ。
It's hard to wake up in the morning after a **long** summer break.

323- ことになる/koto-ni-naru [cp] *it is going to be that ...*

電車の時間が変わることになる。
The train schedule **is going to** change.

324- 本/hon [n] *book*

本は想像力を養うのによい。
Reading **books** nurtures the imagination.

325- どの/dono [adn] *which, what*

どの電車に乗ればいいのかな。
Which train should I take?

326- こちら/kochira [n] *here*

こちらに来て下さい。
Please come **here**.

327- いわゆる/iwayuru [adv] *the so-called*

いわゆるアイドルには興味がない。
I am not interested in **so-called** idols.

328- わ/wa [p] at sentence end; female term

とても嬉^{うれ}しい**わ**。

I am so happy.

329- 夜/yoru [n] *evening, night*

夜^{よる}は電気代^{でんきだい}が安^{やす}くなる。

Electricity is cheaper at **night**.

330- 別/betsu [na-adj] *distinction, different*

リサイクルゴミは**別**^{べつ}の日^ひに出^だす。

We put out recyclable trash on a **different** day.

331- 者/mono [n] *person, people*

係^{かかり}の**者**^{もの}が対応^{たいおう}いたします。

The **person** in charge will take care of you.

332- タイトル/taitoru [n] *title*

その本^{ほん}の**タイトル**は何^{なに}。

What is the **title** of that book?

333- 親/oya [n] *parent, parents*

親^{おや}は介護^{かいご}が必要^{ひつよう}になってきたようだ。

My **parents** seem to be needing more care.

334- 名前/namae [n] *name, full name, given name*

ここに**名前**^{なまえ}を書^かいてください。

Please write down your **name** here.

335- 全部/zenbu [adv] *all, entire*

ごみは**全部**^{ぜんぶ}捨^すてなさい。

Throw away **all** the garbage.

336- 皆さん/minasan [n] *everyone, all*

皆さんのおかげでこのイベントは大成功になりました。

Thanks to **everyone**, this event was a huge success.

337- により/ni-yori [cp] *according to, due to*

新しい税率により、徴収されています。

Tax is being collected **according to** the new tax rate.

338- きれい/kiree [na-adj] *pretty, beautiful, clean*

きれいな色の服を着ると明るい気持ちになる。

Wearing **pretty** colored clothes puts me in a happy mood.

339- 立つ/tatsu [v] *stand up*

乾杯のときは立つ。

Stand up when making a toast.

340- 毎日/mainichi [n] *every day, daily*

ダイエットするには、毎日の運動が欠かせない。

Daily exercise is essential for dieting.

341- 為に/tameni [conj] *for, to one's advantage*

子供の夏休みの宿題の為に朝顔を育てる。

We are growing morning glories **for** my children's summer homework.

342- おいしい/oishii [i-adj] *delicious, sweet*

この地域にはおいしい食べ物が多いね。

This region has a lot of **delicious** food.

343- または/matawa [conj] *or, otherwise*

コーヒーまたは紅茶はがいかがですか。

Would you care for coffee **or** tea?

344- 家族/kazoku [n] *family*

家族旅行に行く。
We are going on a **family** trip.

345- に対する/ni-taisuru [cp] *with regard to, towards*

人に対する敬意を忘れてはならない。
Never forget respect **towards** others.

346- 部分/bubun [n] *portion, section*

おいしい部分を先に食べる。
I eat the yummy **part** first.

347- 一度/ichido [n] *once, on one occasion*

一度試してみるべきだ。
You should try it **once**.

348- 結果/kekka [n] *result, consequence*

病院に電話して検査の結果を聞く。
Call the hospital to get the test **results**.

349- じゃ/ja [conj] *then, so*

じゃ、その時に会おうね。
See you **then**!

350- 状況/jookyoo [n] *state of affairs, circumstance*

今の状況では、いい結果は期待できません。
Under the current **circumstances**, we can't expect a good outcome.

351- 時代/jidai [n] *period, era, those days*

時代によって人の生き方が違う。
People's way of life was different in each **era**.

352- 少ない/sukunai [i-adj] *few, a little, insufficient*

今月は収入が**少ない**。

My income is **low** this month.

353- うまい/umai [i-adj] *skillful, expert, delicious*

彼は本当に運転が**うまい**。

He is a highly **skilled** driver.

354- 覚える/oboeru [v] *memorize, remember*

顔と名前を**覚える**。

Remember the face and the name.

355- 東京/tookyoo [n] *Tokyo*

東京はどこに行っても混んでいる。

Tokyo is crowed wherever you go.

356- てある/te-aru [cp] *has already been done*

私の名前がもう登録し**てある**。

My name **has already been** registered.

357- 続く/tsuzuku [v] *continue, last*

道が遠くまで**続く**。

The road **continues** for a long way.

358- における/ni-okeru [cp] *as for, in*

この分野**における**進歩はすごい。

Much progress has been made **in** this field of study.

359- 俺/ore [pron] *I, me (male term; very casual, rough or arrogant)*

俺は鹿児島生まれだ。

I was born in Kagoshima.

360- 生まれる/umareru [v] *to be born*

もうすぐ子供が**生まれる**。
We are expecting our child to **be born** soon.

361- 父/chichi [n] *one's father*

父は忙しくてあまり家にいません。
My **father** is so busy that he is rarely at home.

362- 確か/tashika [na-adj] *sure, certain, definite*

確かに見たことがある。
I have seen it **for sure**.

363- それぞれ/sorezore [n] *each, respectively*

それぞれ好みがちがう。
Each of us has different tastes.

364- 方法/hoohoo [n] *method, way*

違う**方法**でやってみよう。
Let's try a different **method**.

365- はず/hazu [n] *should be, bound to be*

時間が変わったことは、みんな知っている**はず**です。
They **should** all know that the time has been changed.

366- 説明/setsumee [n] *explanation*

よく**説明**を聞かないとわからない。
I would be lost if I don't listen to the **explanation** carefully.

367- なければいけない/nakereba-ikenai [cp] *have to do, ought to*

この宿題は終わらせ**なければならない**。
I **ought to** complete this homework.

368- 部屋/heya [n] *room, apartment*

部屋を掃除する。

I will clean up my **room**.

369- ちょうど/choodo [adv] *exactly, just*

ちょうど今日が誕生日です。

It **just** happens to be my birthday.

370- 当然/toozen [na-adj] *naural, as a matter of course*

彼が怒ったのも当然だ。

It is only **natural** that he got angry.

371- 大学/daigaku [n] *university, college*

都心から離れた大学に通いたい。

I want to go to a **college** outside the city.

372- ですから/desukara [conj] *so, therefore*

地方ですから交通の便はよくない。

It is a rural area **so** transportation is not so convenient.

373- 実/jitsu [n] *truth, reality*

実は、鍵をなくしてしまいました。

To tell you the **truth**, I have lost my key.

374- 朝/asa [n] *morning*

朝と夜は寒い。

It's chilly in the **morning** and at night.

375- どんどん/dondon [adv] *rapidly, increasingly*

どんどん暗くなる。

It's **rapidly** getting darker.

376- 得る/eru [v] *earn, acquire*

本から知識を得る。

You **acquire** knowledge from books.

377- とにかく/tonikaku [adv] *anyhow, regardless*

とにかく早く始めよう。

Anyhow, let's get started.

378- 選ぶ/erabu [v] *choose, select*

抽選で当選者を選ぶ。

The winner will be **selected** by lottery.

379- 面白い/omoshiroi [i-adj] *interesting, amusing , funny*

コメディ映画は面白い。

Comedy movies are **amusing**.

380- 戻る/modoru [v] *return, turn back*

道を間違ったので元に戻る。

Since I have taken a wrong turn, I am **returning** to the start.

381- 勉強/benkyoo [n] *study*

会計士になる勉強をする。

I am **stud**ying to become an accountant.

382- やめる/yameru [v] *cancel, abolish, stop*

トラブルになることはやめる。

Stop doing things that lead you to trouble.

383- 下/shita [n] *below, bottom, under*

この崖の下は川だから落ちないように気をつけて。

Be careful not to fall as there is a river **below** this cliff.

384- 始める/hajimeru [v] *start, begin*

今度プログラミングの勉強を**始める**ことにしました。

I am going to **start** studying programming.

385- まわり/mawari [n] *surroundings, circumference, around*

道をわたるときは、**まわり**をよく見るようにしなさい。

Pay attention to your **surroundings** when you cross the street.

386- 犬/inu [n] *dog*

犬の方が猫より好きだ。

I prefer **dogs** over cats.

387- 必ず/kanarazu [adv] *always, certainly*

必ず期限までに返します。

I will **certainly** return it by the due date.

388- 残す/nokosu [v] *leave (behind), save*

食べ物をお皿に**残す**のは行儀が悪い。

It is not good manners to **leave** food on your plate.

389- 大事/daiji [na-adj] *important, valuable*

大事なことはメモに書こう。

Write down the **important** things.

390- 嬉しい/ureshii [i-adj] *happy, glad*

今日は上司に褒められて**嬉しい**。

I am **glad** that my boss praised me today.

391- 遊ぶ/asobu [v] *play, enjoy*

公園は子供が**遊ぶ**ための場所だ。

The playground is a place for children to **play**.

392- 理由/riyuu [n] *reason*

理由もなく断られた。

I was denied without a **reason**.

393- 女/onna [n] *female, woman*

女一人で夜道を歩くのは危ない。

It is dangerous for a **woman** to walk on the street alone at night.

394- 簡単/kantan [na-adj] *simple, easy*

算数は二年生までは簡単だ。

Arithmetic is **easy** until the second grade.

395- 始まる/ hajimaru [v] *begin, start*

もうすぐ劇が始まる。

The play is about to **start**.

396- 死ぬ/shinu [v] *die, pass away*

人はみんな死ぬ運命だ。

Everyone is destined to **die**.

397- 今回/konkai [n] *this time*

今回のエピソードは特におもしろかった。

The episode was particularly interesting **this time**.

398- に関する/ni-kansuru [cp] *related to, regarding*

育児に関する相談は経験者に聞くのがよい。

For advice **regarding** raising children, you should ask someone with experience.

399- 人生/jinsee [n]*life*

人生は旅のようだ。

Life is like a journey.

400- 通り/toori [n] *avenue, street*

この**通り**は車が多い。

There is a heavy traffic on this **street**.

401- 内容/naiyoo [n] *contents*

小学生には高度な**内容**です。

The **contents** are too advanced for elementary school students.

402- テレビ/terebi [n] *television, TV program*

テレビが最近つまらなくなってきた。

TV programs have become boring lately.

403- 経験/keeken [n] *experience*

何事も**経験**してみないとわからない。

You won't know what it's like unless you **experience** it.

404- 木/ki [n] *tree, shrub, wood, timber*

庭に大きな**木**がある。

There is a big **tree** in the backyard.

405- 点/ten [n] *spot, point, dot*

点と**点**をつなぐと線になる。

When you connect the **dots**, you make a line.

406- 自然/shizen [n] *nature*

自然の中で子育てをしたい。

I want to raise my children close to **nature**.

407- 音/oto [n] *sound, noise*

どこかからピアノの音が聴こえてくる。

I can hear the **sound** of a piano coming from somewhere.

408- 海/umi [n] *sea, ocean*

今年の夏は海に行きたい。

I want to go to the **sea** this summer.

409- 一応/ichioo [adv] *roughly, for the time being*

一応、メールは出しました。

For the time being, I have sent an email.

410- 与える/ataeru [v] *give, grant, provide*

赤ちゃんにミルクを与える。

I will **give** the baby some milk.

411- 利用/riyoo [n] *use*

このコンピューターは現在利用中です。

This computer is now in **use**.

412- 働く/hataraku [v] *work, labor, function*

外資系の会社で働く。

I **work** for a foreign company.

413- 一杯/ippai [n] *cupful, a glass of*

お水を一杯ください。

Please give me **a glass of** water.

414- 近く/chikaku [n] *near, vicinity*

近くにコンビニがある。

There is a convenience store **nearby**.

415- つまり/ tsumari [adv] *in short, in other words*

つまり、すべて僕の勘違いだった。

In other words, it was all my misunderstanding.

416- 共/tomo [n] *together with, alongside*

彼と共に戦います。

I will fight **alongside** him.

417- 存在/sonzai [n] *existence, being*

宇宙人の存在を信じています。

I believe in the **existence** of aliens.

418- 絶対/zettai [adv] *absolutely*

これは絶対に大事なものです。

This is **absolutely** an important issue.

419- 日本人/nihonjin [n] *Japanese person/people*

日本人はよくおじぎをする。

Japanese people often bow.

420- 大切/taisetsu [na-adj] *important, precious*

大切なものは宝箱に入れておこう。

Keep your **precious** items in a treasure box.

421- 足/ashi [n] *foot*

一日中歩いたので足がいたい。

My **feet** hurt since I walked all day.

422- 切る/ kiru [v] *cut*

はさみでテープを切る。

Cut the tape with scissors.

423- 走る/hashiru [v] *run*

朝走るのが好きです。
I like **run**ning in the morning.

424- 待つ/matsu [v] *wait*

荷物が届くのを待つ。
I am **waiting** for a delivery.

425- 写真/shashin [n] *photograph*

子供の写真をいつも持っている。
I always carry a **photograph** of my children.

426- 子供たち/kodomotachi [n] *children*

子供たちはお年玉を楽しみにしている。
The **children** are looking forward to their *Otoshidama**.
*Otoshidama is a monetary gift given to children by adult relatives
on New Year's Day. The money is presented in special small
envelopes.

427- だんだん/dandan [adv] *gradually*

部屋がだんだん暖かくなってくる。
The room is **gradually** getting warmer.

428- 二つ/futatsu [num] *two*

二つのことを同時にすることはできない。
You can't do **two** things at the same time.

429- 楽しむ/tanoshimu [v] *enjoy*

テレビを見るのを楽しむ。
I **enjoy** watching TV.

430- 五/go [num] *five*

男の子は**五歳**を祝う。

Japanese boys celebrate their **fifth** birthday.

431- 多く/ooku [adv] *many, much*

劇場には**多く**の人がいました。

There were **many** people in the theater.

432- 寝る/neru [v] *sleep*

ふとんよりもベッドで**寝る**のが好きだ。

I like **sleeping** on a bed rather than a futon.

433- 英語/eego [n] *English (language)*

英語は発音が難しい。

English pronunciation is difficult.

434- 決める/kimeru [v] *decide, choose*

待ち合わせの場所を**決める**。

We will **decide** on a place to meet.

435- 忘れる/wasureru [v] *forget*

約束の時間を**忘れる**。

I will probably **forget** the appointment time.

436- 口/kuchi [n] *mouth*

歯医者では大きく**口**を開けないといけない。

You need to open your **mouth** wide at the dentist.

437- 送る/okuru [v] *send, dispatch*

この包みはお母さんに**送る**ものだ。

I am **sending** this package to my mother.

64

438- 姿/sugata [n] *figure, appearance*

好きなキャラクターが姿を現した。

My favorite character made an **appearance**.

439- なくなる/nakunaru [v] *be lost, missing*

公園で帽子がなくなる。

My cap **is lost** in the park.

440- 時期/jiki [n] *time, season, phase*

桜の花が咲く時期だ。

It's the **season** for cherry blossoms to start blooming.

441- 逆/gyaku [na-adj] *reverse, opposite*

車の向きが逆だ。

The car is facing the **opposite** way.

442- 頑張る/ganbaru [v] *persevere, do one's best*

試合で頑張る。

We will **do our best** in the match.

443- 示す/shimesu [v] *show, demonstrate, point out*

プレゼンで例を示す。

I will **show** an example during the presentation.

444- こそ/koso [p] *for sure, be sure (emphasis)*

今度こそ成功しますように。

Let's **be sure** that, this time, we succeed.

445- 人々/hitobito [n] *people, each person*

展示会は人々で混んでいた。

The fair was crowded with **people**.

446- 道/michi [n] *road, path, course*

この道を行けば高速に出ます。
This **road** will take you to the freeway.

447- 有名/yuumee [na-adj] *famous*

レストランで有名な俳優を見た。
I saw a **famous** actor at the restaurant.

448- 思い/omoi [n] *thought, mind*

この小説には特別な思いがある。
I have some specific **thoughts** about this novel.

449- しかも/shikamo [conj] *moreover, nevertheless*

電車が遅れた。しかも、タクシーを待つ長い列があった。
The train was delayed. **Moreover**, there was a long line for the taxi.

450- 難しい/muzukashii [i-adj] *difficult, troublesome*

いじめは難しい問題だ。
Bullying is a **difficult** issue.

451- 彼ら/karera [pron] *they, them*

彼らはチームメイトだ。
They are my teammates.

452- 山/yama [n] *mountain*

富士山は日本で一番高い山です。
Mt. Fuji is the highest **mountain** in Japan.

453- 程度/teedo [n] *degree, grade, level*

この程度の熱なら医者に行かなくてもよい。
You don't need to see a doctor for a fever of this **level**.

454- でない/de-nai [cp] *is not, am not, are not*

それは真実でない。
That **is not** the truth.

455- 願う/negau [v] *desire, wish. beg, pray, hope*

いい結果を願う。
I **hope** for a good result.

456- すでに/sudeni [adv] *already, too late*

すでに知らせは届いている。
We **already** got the notice.

457- 昭和/shoowa [n] *Showa era (12/25/1926 - 1/7/1989)*

昭和時代は、テレビは人気があった。
TV was popular in the **Showa era**.

458- 向かう/mukau [v] *go towards, head out*

車で動物園へ向かう。
We will **head** out **to** the zoo by car.

459- 連れる/tsureru [v] *lead, take (person)*

女の子が大きな犬を連れている。
The girl is **taking** a large dog.

460- 変える/kaeru [v] *change, alter, transform*

規定を変える。
We will **change** the policy.

461- 影響/eekyoo [n] *influence, effect*

日本のポップミュージックはアメリカの影響を受けています。

Japanese pop music has been **influenced** by the U.S.

462- 病院/byooin [n] *hospital*

街には救急病院があります。

There is an emergency **hospital** in the city.

463- 年/toshi [n] *year, years*

年がたつにつれて、私は仕事で忙しくなりました。

As the **years** went by, I became with my work.

464- 花/hana [n] *flower, blossom*

花屋で黄色い花を買おう。

Let's buy yellow **flowers** at the florist.

465- 求める/motomeru [v] *want, wish for, request*

プログラミングの出来る人を求める会社が多い。

Many companies **want** workers with programming skills.

466- 情報/joohoo[n] *information*

新しい情報がある。

I have new **information**.

467- もらう/morau [v] *receive, accept*

プレゼントをもらう。

I **receive** a present.

468- 友人/yuujin [n] *friend*

友人のパーティに行く。

I am going to my **friend**'s party.

469- だめ/dame [na-adj] *no good, useless, in vain*

それはだめだ。

That is **no good**.

470- 経つ/tatsu [v] *pass, lapse*

テストが始まってから十分が経つ。

10 minutes have **passed** since the test began.

471- 先程/sakihodo [n] *a moment ago*

先程お話ししました。

I spoke with you **a moment ago**.

472- 一回/ikkai [n] *once, one round, one time* I

一回福引を引けます。

You get to draw from the lottery **one time**.

473- 十分/juubun [na-adj] *plenty, sufficient*

十分な食料が蓄えられている。

There is **plenty** of food stored away.

474- 小さな/chiisana [adj] *small, tiny*

道の脇に小さな花が咲いている。

There is a **tiny** flower by the sidewalk.

475- 開く/hiraku [v] *open*

お菓子の入っている戸棚を開く。

Open the cabinet with some treats in it.

476- 無人島/mujintoo [n] *deserted island*

一度は無人島に行ってみたい。

I would like to go to a **deserted island** at least once.

477- 続ける/tsuzukeru [v] *continue, keep on*

運動を毎日続ける。

Keep on exercising every day.

478- 重要/juuyoo [n] *important, essential*

重要なところにハイライトをつける。

Highlight the **important** parts.

479- といった/to-itta [cp] *such...as*

アンティーク家具といった古いものに興味がある。

I am interested in **such** things **as** antique furniture.

480- 当たる/ ataru [v] *be hit, strike, win*

抽選で商品が当たる。

Win a prize in the lottery.

481- 近い/chikai [i-adj] *nearby, close*

近い公園に行く。

I go to the **nearby** park.

482- 結婚/kekkon [n] *marriage*

最近は結婚しない人も多い。

Recently, more people are not getting **married**.

483- 認める/mitomeru [v] *recognize, deem*

日本人は電車の中でマナーがいいと認める。

I **recognize** that Japanese people have good manners on the train.

484- これら/ korera [pron] *these*

これらをご自由にお取りください。

Please feel free to take **these**.

485- 歴史/rekishi [n] *history*

古代文明の歴史はおもしろい。

The **history** of ancient civilization is interesting.

486- 増える/fueru [v] *increase*

日本に移民が増える。

Immigration to Japan will **increase**.

487- 音楽/ongaku [n] *music*

好きな音楽は何ですか。

What is your favorite **music**?

488- なければならない/nakere-ba-nara-nai [cp] *have to do, ought to*

仕事で人に会わなければならない。

I **have to** meet some people at work.

489- 外/soto [n] *outside, exterior, open air*

子供は外で遊ばせよう。

Let the children play **outside**.

490- 進む/susumu [v] *go forward, advance*

次のページに進む。

Go to the next page.

491- 起きる/okiru [v] *get up, wake up*

毎朝六時に起きる。

I **wake up** at 6:00 A.M. every morning.

492- 嫌/iya [n] *disagreeable, reluctant*

嫌なことははっきり教えて。

Let me know if you find anything **disagreeable**.

493- 駅/eki [n] *station*

この駅には電車が1日に一回しかこない。
The train comes to this **station** only once a day.

494- いや/iya [interj] *no, why, oh*

いや、それは違うと思うよ。
No, I don't think that's right.

495- はい/hai [interj] *yes, okay*

はい、わかりました。
Yes, I understand.

496- 映画/eega [n] *movie, film*

映画は映画館でみるのがいい。
It more fun to watch **movies** at the theaters.

497- 身/mi [n] *body, oneself*

身の安全が一番だ。
Watching out for **your own** safety is most important.

498- 客/kyaku [n] *guest, customer*

苦情の多い客は困る。
It's hard dealing with a **customer** with a lot of complaints.

499- 質問/shitsumon [n] *question, inquiry*

質問はよく聞いてから答えよう。
Listen to the **question** carefully before you answer.

500- 含む/fukumu [v] *contain, include*

このケーキにはグルテンが含まれている。
This cake **contains** gluten.

501- 地域/chiiki [n] *area, region*

この地域では伝統的な祭りがある。

There is a traditional festival in this **region**.

502- 我が/waga [pron] *my, our, one's own*

我が家では犬を飼っています。

I have a dog in **my** house.

503- どうしても/dooshitemo [adv] *by all means, no matter what*

どうしても仕上げないといけないことがある。

I have something I need to complete, **no matter what**.

504- のに/noni [p] *although, in spite of*

気を付けたのに、また間違えた。

I made a mistake again, **although** I was being very careful.

505- 娘/musume [n] *my/our daughter, unmarried girl*

娘に着物を買う。

I am buying a kimono for my **daughter**.

506- 見せる/miseru [v] *show, display*

新しい車を見せる。

I will **show** you my new car.

507- 一日/ichinichi [n] *one day*

一日ですべてのテストを受けなければならない。

You must take all the tests in **one day**.

508- 今年/kotoshi [n] *this year*

今年は日本語を勉強します。

I will study Japanese **this year**.

509- 平成/heesee [n] *Heisei era (1/8/1989-4/30/2019)*

平成の時代は経済が停滞した。

The economy stagnated during the **Heisei era**.

510- 図/zu [n] *drawing, diagram, figure*

参考資料の図をご覧ください。

Please see the **diagram** in the reference material.

511- 紹介/shookai [n] *introduction, referral*

友達に彼を紹介してもらった。

My friend **introduce**d me to him.

512- 合わせる/awaseru [v] *match, join together*

靴下の右と左を合わせる。

Match the right and left socks.

513- 安い/yasui [i-adj] *cheap, inexpensive*

安いチケットが手にはいった。

I got a **cheap** ticket.

514- 夢/yume [n] *dream*

私には大きな夢があります。

I have a big **dream**.

515- つらい/tsurai [i-adj] *(emotionally) hard, heart-breaking*

二日酔いで、つらい。

I am having a **hard** time with a hangover.

516- 規定/kitee [n] *regulation, provision, rule*

規定によって、赤ちゃんはジェットコースターに乗れない。

According to the **rules**, infants are not allowed on the roller coasters.

517- どちら/dochira [pron] *which direction, where, which one*

どちらの道が正しいかわからない。

I'm not sure **which** is the right way.

518- 中心/chuushin [n] *center, core*

世界の中心はどこだろうか。

I wonder where the **center** of the world is.

519- 起こる/okoru [v] *occur, happen*

次から次へと問題が起こる。

Problems **occur** one after another.

520- 我々/wareware [pron] *we, our, us*

我々の先祖はどこから来たのだろう。

Where did **our** ancestors come from?

521- 立てる/tateru [v] *to stand up, set up*

看板を立てる。

Set up a signboard.

522- 最も/mottomo [adv] *most*

最もスコアの高い人が優勝だ。

Whoever gets the **highest** score is the winner.

523- 色/iro [n] *color*

好きな色は何。

What is your favorite **color**?

524- 探す/sagasu [v] *search for, seek, find*

なくした物を探す。

Find your lost items.

525- ちゃんと/chanto [adv] *diligently, perfectly*

ちゃんと仕事をしなさい。
Do your work **diligently**.

526- 興味/kyoomi [n] *interest*

科学に興味がある。
I have an **interest** in science.

527- 三つ/mittsu [num] *three*

クッキーを三つずつお皿にのせる。
Put **three** cookies on each plate.

528- ほしい/hoshii [i-adj] *want, wish for*

こちらの仕事を先にしてほしい。
I **want** you to take care of this task first.

529- 売る/uru [v] *sell*

ガレージセールで自転車を売る。
I will **sell** my bicycle at a garage sale.

530- 変化/henka [n] *change, transformation*

季節の変化に気づく。
Feel the **change** of the seasons.

531- 印象/inshoo [n] *impression*

いい印象の人だった。
He left a nice **impression** on me.

532- 作品/sakuhin [n] *work*

展覧会で作品を見る。
See a **work** of art at the exhibition.

533- でございます/de-gozai-masu [cp] *be (formal)*

こちらが東大寺の大仏でございます。
This **is** the Great Buddha of Todaiji.

534- 参加/sanka [n] *participation*

ミュージアムのイベントに参加した。
I **participated** in a museum event.

535- 夏/natsu [n] *summer*

夏になったら海に行こう。
Let's go to the beach in **summer**.

536- よる/yoru [v] *due to, depend on*

移動時間は道路状況による。
The travel time depends on traffic.

537- 理解/rikai [n] *understanding, comprehension*

小さい子供は曜日が理解できない。
It's hard for small children to **understand** the days of the week.

538- 事件/jiken [n] *incident, event, affair*

平和な街で事件がおきた。
An **incident** occurred in a peaceful town.

539- 中国/chuugoku [n] *China*

中国はとても広い国だ。
China is a large country.

540- ずつ/zutsu [p] *each, by, at a time*

バイオリンが少しずつ上手になる。
My violin is improving little **by** little.

541- 母親/hahaoya [n] *mother*

母親が赤ちゃんに母乳を与えている。

A **mother** is nursing her baby.

542- 取り敢えず/toriaezu [adv] *for the time being, for now*

取り敢えず、問題を上司に報告する。

For the time being, I will report the matter to my boss.

543- ところが/tokoroga [p. conj] *by the way, incidentally*

旅行を楽しみにしていた。ところが、空港でお父さんに会ったよ。

I was looking forward to the trip. **By the way**, I met your father at the airport.

544- 目的/mokuteki [n] *purpose, objective*

外国語を学ぶ目的は何ですか。

What is your **purpose** of learning a foreign language?

545- 様々/samazama [na-adj] *various*

様々なテーマについて話し合った。

We discussed **various** topics.

546- 答える/kotaeru [v] *answer, reply*

質問に答える。

Answer the question.

547- 過ごす/sugosu [v] *pass, spend (time)*

休みの日は家で過ごす。

I **spend** my day off at home.

548- 一方/ippoo [conj] *on the other hand*

一方、うさぎは昼寝をした。

On the other hand, the rabbit took a nap.

549- 病気/byooki [n] *illness, disease*

早く病気が良くなるよう祈っています。

Wishing you a fast recovery from your **illness**.

550- 心配/shinpai [n] *worry, anxiety*

心配いりません。大丈夫です。

No need to **worry**. Everything's okay.

551- それでも/soredemo [conj] *nevertheless, even so*

それでも、母親は子供が心配だ。

Even so, mothers worry about their children.

552- イメージ/imeeji [n] *image*

企業イメージはマーケティングに重要だ。

A corporate **image** is important for marketing.

553- 笑い/warai [n] *laughter*

笑いは伝染する。

Laughter is contagious.

554- 午後/gogo [n] *afternoon, P.M.*

午後になったら買い物に行く。

I will go shopping in the **afternoon**.

555- 動く/ugoku [v] *move, operate*

ドローンはリモートで動く。

Drones are **operated** remotely.

556- 主人/shujin [n] *head, husband*

主人はよく出張にいきます。

My husband often goes on business trips.

557- 加える/ kuwaeru [v] *add, sum up*

スープに塩を加える。
Add some salt to the soup.

558- 困る/komaru [v] *be bothered, be troubled*

隣人の騒音で困る。
We **are bothered** by the neighbor's noise.

559- 取れる/ toreru [v] *come off, be removed*

ワインのシミが取れる。
Wine stains can **come off**.

560- 環境/kankyoo [n] *environment*

自然環境について考える。
Contemplate the natural **environment**.

561- 対応/taioo [v] *deal with, respond to*

お客様からの問い合わせに対応する。
Respond to customer inquiries.

562- 比べる/kuraberu [v] *compare*

クッキーの大きさを比べる。
Compare the size of the cookies.

563- 高校/kookoo [n] *high school*

高校でスペイン語を学んだ。
I learned Spanish in **High School**.

564- 食事/shokuji [n] *meal*

食事の前に手を洗う。
Wash your hands before your **meal**.

565- 引く/hiku [v] *pull, draw (attention)*

ドアの取手を引く。
Pull the door handle.

566- 辺/hen [n] *area, vicinity*

この辺はホテルが多い。
There are many hotels in this **area**.

567- 要するに/yoosuruni [adv] *simply put, after all*

要するに、私は肉料理が好きじゃありません。
Simply put, I don't like eating meat dishes.

568- 離れる/hanareru [v] *be separated, stay away from*

展示物から離れる。
Stay away from the exhibits.

569- 火/hi [n] *fire, flame*

火は人類の最初の発明だ。
Fire is the first invention of mankind.

570- 実施/jisshi (suru) [v] *enforce, implement, conduct*

リサイクルキャンペーンを実施する。
We are **conducting** a recycling campaign.

571- 今後/kongo [n] *from now on, hereafter*

この建物には今後入らないようにしてください。
From now on, please do not enter this building.

572- 社会/shakai [n] *society, public, community, social studies*

社会のために役立ちたい。
I would like to contribute to **society**.

573- 練習/renshuu [n] *practice*

サッカーの練習をする。
I will **practice** soccer.

574- 使用/shiyoo [n] *use*

携帯の使用は禁止されている。
The **use** of mobile phones is prohibited.

575- 超える/ koeru [v] *cross over, exceed*

スピード六十キロを超える。
Its speed **exceed**s sixty kilometers per hour.

576- 図る/hakaru [v] *plot, attempt*

新しい対策を図る。
We will **attempt** to put in place new measures.

577- 企業/kigyoo [n] *enterprise, corporation*

大企業で働く。
I work for a large **corporation**.

578- 奴/yatsu [n] *fellow, guy*

彼はいい奴だ。
He is a good **guy**.

579- はっきり/hakkiri [adv] *clearly, distinctly*

はっきりと意見を言う。
State your opinion **clearly**.

580- 怖い/kowai [i-adj] *scary, frightening*

おばけやしきは怖い。
Haunted houses are **scary**.

581- 例/ree [n] *example*

例をあげて説明する。
Explain with **examples**.

582- 絵/e [n] *picture, painting, drawing*

風景の絵が好きだ。
I like landscape **paintings**.

583- 思い出す/omoidasu [v] *recall, remember*

この場所に来ると子供のころを思い出す。
I **remember** my childhood when I come to this place.

584- に関して/ni-kanshi-te [cp] *regarding, with regard to*

子育てに関しては妻に任せている。
With regard to parenting, I leave that to my wife.

585- 酒/sake [n] *rice wine, alcohol*

正月にお酒を飲む。
Drink **sake** during the New Year holidays.

586- 原因/gen'in [n] *cause*

事故の原因を調べる。
Investigate the **cause** of the accident.

587- お前/omae [pron] *you (colloquial)*

お前と俺は子供の時からの友達だ。
You and I have been friends since childhood.

588- 守る/mamoru [v] *protect, keep*

子供を津波から守る。
Protect children from the tsunami.

589- 小学校/shoogakkoo [n] *elementary school, grade school*

近所の**小学校**で運動会がある。

There is an athletic day at a nearby **elementary school**.

590- 回る/ mawaru [v] *turn, revolve*

メリーゴーラウンドが早く**回る**。

The merry-go-round **turns** fast.

591- 広い/hiroi [i-adj *spacious, vast, wide*

この学校の校庭は**広い**。

This school has **spacious** grounds.

592- 猫/neko [n] *cat*

猫に引っかかれた。

I was scratched by the **cat**.

593- 向こう/mukoo [n] *opposite side, over there*

虹の**向こう**には何があるのだろう。

I wonder what is **over** the rainbow.

594- 同時/dooji [n] *simultaneous, same time*

このシステムでは、同じファイルに**同時**にアクセスできます。

This system allows **simultaneous** access to the same file.

595- 調べる/ shiraberu [v] *investigate, search*

図書館で本を**調べる** 。

Search for books in the library.

596- のぼる/noboru [v] *ascend, rise*

朝、太陽が**のぼる**のを見るのが好きだ。

I like watching the sun **rise** in the morning.

597- 六/roku [num] *six*

一ダースの半分は六だ。
Half of one dozen is **six**.

598- のみ/nomi [p] *only*

このイベントは大人のみ入場できます。
Only adults can enter this event.

599- 向ける/mukeru [v] *turn, point*

植物を太陽に向ける。
Turn the plant to the sun.

600- 落ちる/ochiru [v] *fall down, drop*

りんごが木から落ちる。
Apples **fall** from the tree.

601- だが/daga [conj] *but, however, yet*

急いで仕事をした。だが、まだ終わらない。
I have been working quickly. **But** I'm still not done.

602- 決まる/kimaru [v] *be decided, be settled*

この試合で優勝が決まる。
The victor will **be decided** by this game.

603- 起こす/okosu [v] *wake up*

朝、子どもを起こす。
I **wake up** my child in the morning.

604- 場/ba [n] *place, occasion*

お祝いの場で言葉を述べる。
On the **occasion** of this celebration, please allow me to offer a few words.

605- いずれ/izure [adv] *eventually, anyhow, sooner or later*

いずれ、その日が来る。
Eventually, the day will come.

606- ホテル/hoteru [n] *hotel*

あのホテルは四つ星だ。
That's a four-star **hotel**.

607- 対象/taishoo [n] *target, object of, subject of*

このイベントは小さな子供が対象だ。
This event is **aimed at** small children.

608- 打つ/utsu [v] *hit, strike*

ラケットで球を打つ。
Hit the ball with the racket.

609- 以前/izen [n] *ago, since, before*

以前、その映画を観たことがあります。
I have seen that movie **before**.

610- 夫/otto [n] *husband*

大学で夫に出会った。
I met my **husband** in college.

611- 確認/kakunin [n] *confirmation, verification*

確認のメールをもらう。
I will get a **confirmation** e-mail.

612- 数/kazu [n] *number*

小さい子供には数の概念がない。
Small children do not have the **concept** of numbers.

613- 意見/iken [n] *opinion, comment*

意見はわかりやすく言うのが重要だ。

It's important to state your **opinion** clearly.

614- 割と/warito [adv] *relatively, comparatively, rather*

この車は割と安かったです。

This car was **relatively** cheap.

615- 大丈夫/daijoobu [na-adj] *safe, alright*

彼はころんだけど大丈夫だった。

He fell, but he was **alright**.

616- 通う/kayou [v] *commute, attend*

毎週レッスンに通う。

I **attend** lessons every week.

617- 申し上げる/mooshiageru [v] *say, state, express (humble)*

皆さまに感謝を申し上げる。

I would like to **express** my appreciation to all of you.

618- 可能性/kanoosee [n] *possibility, likelihood*

給料が上がる可能性は高いです。

There is a good **possibility** that I will be getting a raise.

619- 述べる/noberu [v] *state, mention, express*

本についての感想を述べる。

I will **express** my thoughts about the book.

620- 是非/zehi [adv] *certainly, please, by all means, definitely*

是非、我が家に来てください。

Please do come by my home.

621- さえ/sae [p] *even, if only*

高齢者でさえ、そのテーマパークは楽しめる。

Even elderly people can enjoy that theme park.

622- 三人/sannin [n] *three people*

三人乗りの自転車は幅がひろい。

Three-seated bicycles are wide.

623- 料理/ryoori [n] *cooking, cuisine*

フランス料理が大好きです。

I love French **cuisine**.

624- 一部/ichibu [n] *one part, some*

一部の人は同意しなかった。

Some people did not agree.

625- きっと/kitto [adv] *surely, almost certainly*

きっといい事が起こるよ。

I am **certain** that good things will happen.

626- どうして/dooshite [adv] *why?, for what reason*

どうして私は行ってはいけないの。

Why can't I go?

627- 歌う/utau [v] *sing*

カラオケで歌うのが好きです。

I like **singing** at karaoke.

628- なお/nao [adv] *furthermore, in addition*

なお、収益の一部はチャリティーに寄付されます。

In addition, part of the proceeds will be donated to charity.

629- 幾つ/ikutsu [adv] *how many?, how old?*

パーティには椅子が幾つ必要ですか。

How many chairs do we need for the party?

630- ぞ/zo [p] *sentence end: adds force, command*

絶対に頑張るぞ。

I will absolutely do my best!

631- 新聞/shinbun [n] *newspaper*

最近は新聞を読んでいない。

I have not been reading **newspapers** recently.

632- 気付く/kizuku [n] *notice, realize*

忘れ物に気付く。

I **realize** that I have left something behind.

633- 歌/uta [n] *song*

一番好きな歌は何ですか。

What is your favorite **song**?

634- 開ける/akeru [v] *open*

窓を開ける。

I **open** the window.

635- お互い/otagai [n] *mutual, each other*

お互いに助け合おう。

Let's help **each other**.

636- 着る/kiru [v] *wear*

学校の制服を着る。

We **wear** the school uniform.

637- 違い/chigai [n] *difference, discrepancy*

味の違いがよくわからない。

I can't tell the **difference** in flavor.

638- しっかり/shikkari [adv] *firmly, securely*

シートベルトをしっかりするように。

Put on your seat belt **securely**.

639- 過ぎる/sugiru [v] *pass through, elapse, be over*

冬が過ぎるのを待っています。

I'm waiting for the winter to **be over**.

640- 記憶/kioku [n] *memory, remembrance*

記憶があやふやだ。

My **memory** is fuzzy.

641- 思い出/omoide [n] *memory, reminiscence*

子供の頃の思い出を話す。

Talk about childhood **memories**.

642- しばらく/shibaraku [adv] *for a while*

しばらく練習をしていない。

I have not practiced **for a while**.

643- 基本的/kihonteki [na-adj] *fundamental, standard*

これは基本的な英語コースです。

This is a **standard** English course.

644- 四月/shigatsu [n] *April*

四月から新学期が始まる。

The new school year starts in **April**.

645- 君/kimi [pron] *you, buddy, pal*

あとで君に電話するよ。
I will call **you** later.

646- 笑う/warau [v] *laugh, smile*

コントを見て笑う。
Laugh at the skit.

647- いくら/ikura [adv] *how much? How many?*

これはいくらですか。
How much is this?

648- 魚/sakana [n] *fish*

豊洲で魚を買う。
Buy **fish** at the *Toyosu market**.
*Toyosu Maket is one of the largest fish markets in the world.
Located in Koto-ward, Tokyo, it is a popular tourist spot.

649- 旅行/ ryokoo [n] *travel, trip*

ドライブ旅行に行きます。
I am going on a road **trip**.

650- 父親/chichioya [n] *father*

僕は父親に似ています。
I look like my **father**.

651- どれ/dore [pron] *which*

どれにしますか。
Which one will you take?

652- 見付ける/mitsukeru [v] *discover, find, locate*

探し物を**見付ける**。

I will **find** my lost item.

653- 関わる/kakawaru [v] *concern, be involved*

事件に**関わる**。

I will **be getting involved** in the incident.

654- 無理/muri [na-adj] *unreasonable, impossible*

無理なお願いをしてすみません。

I am sorry for making such an **unreasonable** request.

655- 健康/kenkoo [n] *health*

あなたの**健康**が最も重要です。

Your **health** is the most important.

656- 味/aji [n] *flavor*

それはなに**味**のソースですか。

What **flavor** is the sauce?

657- 深い/fukai [i-adj] *deep*

この 湖 は**深い**。

This lake is **deep**.

658- 伝える/tsutaeru [v] *convey, communicate*

人々にメッセージを**伝える**。

Convey a message to the public.

659- 自由/ jiyuu [n] *freedom, liberty*

自由の女神を見に行く。

I am going to see the Statue of **Liberty**.

660- 集まる/atsumaru [v] *gather, collect*

人々が葬儀に集まる。

People **gather** at the funeral.

661- 戦争/sensoo [n] *war*

二十世紀は戦争が多かった。

There were many **war**s in the twentieth century.

662- 流れる/nagareru [v] *stream, flow*

歩道に雨水が流れる。

Rainwater **stream**s down the sidewalk.

663- 男性/dansee [n] *man, male*

男性用のトイレはどこですか。

Where is the **men**'s bathroom?

664- 電車/densha [n] *train*

電車が時間通りに来た。

The **train** arrived on time.

665- 進める/susumeru [v] *promote, proceed, go forward with*

環境プロジェクトを進める。

We will **go forward with** the environmental project.

666- 含める/fukumeru [v] *include*

決算に子会社を含める。

Include subsidiaries in the financial statements.

667- 致す/itasu [v] *to do (humble)*

その仕事は、私が致します。

I would like to **do** that task.

668- 着く/tsuku [v] *arrive, sit on (seat)*

十一時までに着く予定だ。

I expect to **arrive** by eleven o'clock.

669- 厳しい/kibishii [i-adj] *severe, strict*

私の学校は規則が厳しい。

My school has **strict** rules.

670- 女の子/onnanoko [n] *girl*

女の子の服を買うのは楽しい。

It's fun to shop for **girls'** clothes.

671- パソコン/pasokon [n] *personal computer*

デスクトップのパソコンを買った。

I bought a desktop **computer**.

672- おる/oru* [v] *be, exist (humble)*

私はまだここにおります。

I **am** still here.

*The phrase "oru" is usually used in its extended polite form of "orimasu".

673- 活動/katsudoo [n] *action, activity*

週末はボランティア活動をする。

I participate in volunteer **activities** on weekends.

674- 不安/fuan [n] *anxiety, insecurity*

余震に不安があります。

I have **anxiety** about the aftershocks.

675- 三十分/sanjuppun [n] *30 minutes*

三十分で東京駅に着く。

You will arrive at Tokyo Station in **30 minutes**.

676- 限り/kagiri [n] *limit, extent*

クラスの人数には限りがあります。

There is a **limit** to the class size.

677- いらっしゃる/irassharu [v] *go, be (honorific)*

先生がもうすぐいらっしゃる。

Our teacher will **be** here soon.

678- 可能/kanoo [n] *potential, feasible*

この計画は可能ですか。

Is this plan **feasible**?

679- 可愛い/kawaii [i-adj] *cute, adorable*

私の子犬は可愛いです。

My puppy is **adorable**.

680- 際/sai [n] *when, in case of, on the occasion of,*

部屋に入る際は靴を脱いでください。

Please remove your shoes **when** you enter the room.

681- 途中/tochuu [n] *on the way, en route*

まだ道の途中です。

I am still **on my way**.

682- 研究/kenkyuu [n] *study, research*

遺伝子の研究が進歩する。

Progress has been made in genetic **research**.

683- 様子/yoosu [n] *state of affairs, situation*

様子を見にいこう。
Let's go check the **situation**.

684- ものすごい/monosugoi [i-adj] *terrible*

今年はものすごい台風が来ました。
We had **terrible** typhoons this year.

685- 合う/au [v]*fit, suit*

そのサンダルはドレスによく合う。
The sandals **suit** the dress well.

686- 済む/sumu [v] *finish, completed*

歯の治療が一回で済む。
My dental treatment will be **completed** in just one visit.

687- 通る/ tooru [v] *go by, pass through*

この細い道を通る時は気をつけて。
Be careful when you **pass through** this lane.

688- 大人/otona [n] *adult*

大人2枚、子供1枚のチケットを買う。
Purchase tickets for two **adults** and one child.

689- 期待/kitai [n] *expectation, anticipation*

彼は昇進への高い期待を持っている。
He has high **expectations** for a promotion.

690- 事実/jijitsu [n] *fact, truth, reality*

事実はそのうち明らかになる。
The **truth** will come to light soon.

691- せい/see [n] *resulting from, because of*

天気のせいで、延期になった。

It was postponed **because of** the weather.

692- 一年/ichinen [n] *one year*

一年で日本語が上手になった。

My Japanese has improved a lot in **one year**.

693- 一体/ittai [adv] *What on earth...? What the heck...?*

それは一体何。

What on earth is that?

694- 島/shima [n] *island*

日本には小さな島が多くあります。

There are many small **islands** in Japan.

695- 描く/egaku [v] *draw, paint, sketch*

想像で絵を描く。

I **draw** using my imagination.

696- 驚く/odoroku [v] *be surprised, be astonished*

物音に驚く。

I **am surprised** by the noise.

697- 動物/doobutsu [n] *animal*

動物園で動物を見るのが好きです。

I like watching **animals** at the zoo.

698- 何度/nando [n] *how many times?*

週に何度買い物をしますか。

How many times a week do you go shopping?

97

699- 元々/motomoto [adv] *originally, by nature*

私は元々料理が好きじゃない。

By nature, cooking is not my thing.

700- 素晴らしい/subarashii [i-adj] *wonderful, splendid*

素晴らしいミュージカルだった。

The musical was **wonderful**.

701- 座る/suwaru [v] *sit*

ヨガの座るポーズは瞑想にいい。

Yoga's **sitting** pose is good for meditation.

702- 定める/sadameru [v] *decide, furnish*

町内会の決まりを定める。

We **decide on** the rules for the neighborhood association.

703- 機会/kikai [n] *chance, opportunity*

これは町に貢献する素晴らしい機会だ。

This is a good **opportunity** to make a contribution to the town.

704- 楽しみ/tanoshimi [n] *enjoyment, hobby, look forward to*

孫が生まれるのが楽しみだ。

I am **looking forward to** having a grandchild.

705- 考え/kangae [n] *thought, opinion, idea*

君と僕の考えは違う。

We have different **ideas**.

706- 信じる/shinjiru [v] *believe, trust*

君の話を信じる。

I **believe** your story.

707- たまたま/tamatama [adv] *by chance, accidentally*

たまたま抽選に当たった。
I won the lottery **by chance**.

708- 古い/furui [i-adj] *old, obsolete*

そのネットワークシステムは古いです。
The network system is **obsolete**.

709- 面/men [n] *face, mask*

夏祭りでお面を買った。
I bought a **mask** at a summer festival.

710- さ/sa [p] *ness (suffix indicating degree)*

その子猫は可愛さが違う。
The **cuteness** of this kitten is unique.

711- 三月/sangatsu [n] *March*

三月にはひな祭りがある。
The *Hinamatsuri** festival is in **March**.

*Hinamatsuri, also known as Doll's Day or Peach Festival, is celebrated on March 3rd every year. A set of ornamental dolls, portraying a Heian period wedding, are displayed on a multi-tiered doll stand covered by a red carpet.

712- ただし/tadashi [conj] *however, provided that*

ただし、暗くなる前に帰ること。
Provided that you return before dusk.

713- 常/tsune [adv] *always, usually*

常に子供の健康に気をつける。
Always take care of your child's health.

714- つもり/tsumori [n] *intention*

そんな**つもり**ではなかった。
That was not my **intention**.

715- 考え方/kangaekata [n] *way of thinking*

違う**考え方**を知るのはいいことだ。
It's good to be aware of different **ways of thinking**.

716- ニュース/nyuusu [n] *news*

テレビで地震の**ニュース**を見た。
I watched the **news** about the earthquake on TV.

717- 意識/ishiki [n] *consciousness, awareness*

安全への**意識**を高める。
Promote safety **awareness**.

718- 元/moto [n] *origin, source*

発明の**元**は失敗にあった。
The **origin** of the invention was in a failure.

719- 行動/koodoo [n] *action, behavior*

大人と子供の**行動**は違う。
The **behaviors** of adults and children are different.

720- 低い/hikui [i-adj] *low (quality, degree, position)*

今日は気温が**低い**。
The temperature is **low** today.

721- びっくり/bikkuri [adv] *be surprised, be frightened*

知らせに**びっくり**した。
I **was surprised** by the news.

722- 作り方/tsukurikata [n] *way of making, recipe*

パンケーキの**作り方**が箱に書いてある。

A pancake **recipe** is on the box.

723- 元気/genki [na-adj] *lively, energetic, well*

あなたが**元気**でありますように。

I wish you **well**.

724- 現れる/arawareru [v] *appear*

雲の合間に虹が**現れる**。

A rainbow **appears** between the clouds.

725- 聞こえる/kikoeru [v] *be heard, be audible, can hear*

鳥の鳴き声が**聞こえる**。

I **can hear** birds sing.

726- 曲/kyoku [n] *song, music*

ジャズの**曲**が流れているカフェが好きだ。

I like cafes with Jazz **music**.

727- 過去/kako [n] *the past*

過去について話をするのはやめよう。

Let's not talk about **the past**.

728- やっと/yatto [adv] *at last, just, barely, finally*

やっとにきびがきれいになった。

My acne has **finally** cleared up.

729- 思える/omoeru [v] *seem, appear likely*

それは夢のように**思える**。

It **seems** like a dream.

730- 明らか/akiraka [na-adj] *obvious, evident*

これは**明らかな**間違いだ。

This is an **obvious** mistake.

731- つつ/tsutsu [p] *while*

前の単元の復習をし**つつ**、新しい単元も学習しよう。

Let's learn the new chapter **while** reviewing the last chapter.

732- 土地/tochi [n] *lot, soil, locality*

この**土地**は昔は田んぼだった。

This **lot** used to be a rice field.

733- 振り返る/furikaeru [v] *look back, turn around*

たまには過去を**振り返る**のもよい。

Sometimes, it's good to **look back** on the past.

734- 初め/hajime [n] *beginning, first*

初めての時は誰でも不安だ。

Everyone is anxious when it is the **first** time.

735- 評価/hyooka [n] *evaluation, assessment*

厳しい**評価**を受けた。

I received a hard **assessment**.

736- 息子/musuko [n] *son*

息子がもうすぐ二十歳になります。

My **son** is turning twenty years old soon.

737- 限る/kagiru [v] *limit, be restricted*

このゴルフコースの使用は会員に**限る**。

Use of this golf course **is limited** to members.

738- 似る/niru [v] *resemble, be similar*

子供は親に**似る**ものだ。

Children **resemble** their parents.

739- 悲しい/kanashii [i-adj] *sad, sorrowful*

愛犬が死んでしまって**悲し**い。

I am **saddened** by the death of my pet dog.

740- 雨/ame [n] *rain*

昨日の夜からの**雨**で水たまりができている。

The **rain** from last night has made puddles.

741- 自分達/jibuntachi [n] *ourselves*

キャンプでは食べ物を**自分達**で作ろう。

Let's make the food at camp **ourselves**.

742- 詳しい/kuwashii [n] *detailed, knowing very well*

詳しい情報はネットで調べよう。

Search for **detailed** information on the Internet.

743- 二十一世紀/nijuuisseeki [n] *21st century*

二十一世紀にはテクノロジーが進むだろう。

Technologies will advance in the **21st century**.

744- ひどい/hidoi [i-adj] *cruel, severe, extreme*

今日は頭痛が**ひどい**。

I have a **severe** headache today.

745- 昨日/kinoo [n] *yesterday*

昨日は飲みすぎた。

I had too much drink **yesterday**.

746- 下りる/oriru [v] *descend, go down, get off*

急な階段を**下りる**。
Go down the steep stairs.

747- メール/meeru [n] *email*

一日に百件以上の**メール**が届く。
I get more than one hundred **emails** a day.

748- 喜ぶ/yorokobu [v] *be delighted*

孫がおもちゃに**喜ぶ**。
My grandchild **is delighted** with the toys.

749- 便利/benri [na-adj] *convenient, handy*

駅にコンビニがあるのは**便利**だ。
It is **convenient** having a convenience store in the station.

750- 迎える/mukaeru [v] *go out to meet, welcome, approach*

門のところでお客様を**迎える**。
I **welcome** my guest at the gate.

751- 耳/mimi [n] *ear*

はずかしくて**耳**が赤くなった。
My **ears** turned red from embarrassment.

752- 表現/hyoogen [n] *expression, presentation*

気持ちを**表現**するのは難しい。
It's hard to **express** feelings.

753- 動き/ugoki [n] *movement, development*

株式市場の**動き**が気になる。
I am concerned about the **movement** in the stock market.

754- 注意/chuui [n] *caution, attention*

車を運転する時はスピードに注意しなさい。
Pay **attention** to your speed when you are driving.

755- では/deha [conj] *then, so, well then*

では、そろそろ行きましょう。
Well then, it's time to go.

756- てあげる/te-ageru [cp] *do something for somebody*

お母さん、誕生日プレゼントを買ってあげる。
Mom, I will **buy** you a gift **for** your birthday.

757- 雰囲気/fun'iki [n] *mood, ambience, aura, atmosphere*

このカフェは雰囲気がいい。
This café has a nice **atmosphere**.

758- 立場/tachiba [n] *standpoint, position*

反対の立場から発言する。
State an opinion from an opposing **standpoint**.

759- 基づく/motozuku [v] *be based on, to originate from*

過去の判例に基づく判決だ。
The judgement was **based on** past cases.

760- ことがある/kotoga-aru [cp] *has occurred to, happens on occasions, to have done*

その写真を見たことがある。
I **have seen** that picture before.

761- 痛い/itai [i-adj] *painful, sore*

重い荷物を運んだので腰が痛い。

My back is **sore** from carrying heavy bags.

762- 辺り/atari [n] *area, vicinity, nearby*

この辺りは劇場が多い。

There are a lot of theaters in this **area**.

763- てやる/te-yaru [cp] *do something for somebody (from a position of seniority, arrogance)*

子供の宿題を手伝ってやる。

I'll **help** my kids with their homework.

764- 将来/shoorai [n] *future, prospects*

将来の夢は飛行士になることです。

My **future** dream is to become an aviator.

765- 乗せる/noseru [v] *place on, give a ride*

彼女をバイクに乗せる。

I **give** my girlfriend **a ride** on my bike.

766- 自転車/jitensha [n] *bicycle*

自転車による事故が増えている。

The number of accidents caused by **bicycles** is increasing.

767- 白い/shiroi [i-adj] *white*

白いシャツを汚さないように気をつけてください。

Be careful not to stain your **white** shirts.

768- 川/kawa [n] *river, stream*

昔の人は川で洗濯をした。

A long time ago, people washed their clothes in the **river**.

769- 用いる/mochiiru [v] *use, utilize*

クラスで新しいカリキュラムを用いる。

We are **using** a new curriculum in class.

770- 隣り/tonari [n] *next to, next door*

新しい家族が隣りに引っ越してきた。

A new family has moved in **next door**.

771- 普段/fudan [adj] *usual, everyday*

普段の服装のまま出かける。

I'll just go out in my **usual** clothes.

772- 法律 /hooritsu [n] *law*

法律は国によって違う。

Laws vary from country to country.

773- 冬/fuyu [n] *winter*

まだ冬の雪が積もったままだ。

We still have some snow piled up from **winter**.

774- 具体的/gutaiteki [na-adj] *concrete, specific*

具体的な説明がないとよくわからない。

I can't comprehend this without a **specific** explanation.

775- もと/moto [n] *under*

教授のもとで研究を続ける。

I will continue my research **under** my professor.

776- 発生／hassee [n] *incidence, occurrence*

竜巻の発生が報告されました。

The **occurrence** of a tornado has been reported.

777- 繰り返す／kurikaesu [v] *repeat*

息子は同じ遊びを繰り返すのが好きだ。

My son likes to play his favorite games **repeatedly**.

778- 泣く／naku [v] *cry, weep*

下の子はよく泣く。

My youngest child **cries** a lot.

779- 七／shichi [num] *seven*

七人家族なのでミニバンが必要だ。

With a family of **seven**, I need a minivan to carry them all.

780- 手紙／tegami [n] *letter*

手紙に気持ちを書く。

I will write down my feelings in a **letter**.

781- 出かける／dekakeru [v] *go out, depart*

車で出かけることが多い。

I often **go out** by car.

782- 努力／doryoku [n] *effort, endeavor*

努力が報われるといいね。

I hope your **efforts** will be rewarded.

783- 増加／zooka [n] *increase, addition*

高齢者の人口が増加する。

The elderly population is **increasing**.

784- 判断/handan [n] *judgement, decision*

上司に**判断**を仰ぐ。

Ask your boss for a **decision**.

785- 両親/ryooshin [n] *parents, both parents*

両親に長生きしてほしい。

I hope my **parents** have long lives.

786- 残念/zannen [na-adj] *disappointing, regrettable*

残念な結果に終わった。

The outcome was **disappointing**.

787- おそらく/osoraku [adv] *perhaps, likely, probably*

彼は**おそらく**時間をまちがえたのだろう。

He **probably** had the wrong time.

788- 家庭/katee [n] *home, household*

家庭に仕事を持ち込まないのがルールです。

We have a rule that we should not bring our work **home**.

789- 払う/harau [v] *pay, brush off*

クレジットカードで代金を**払う**。

Pay by credit card.

790- つながる/tsunagaru [v] *be connected, lead to*

ソーシャルメディアで友達と**つながる**。

Connect with friends on social media.

791- 船/fune [n] *ship, boat, vessel*

湾岸で**船**のパーティを開く。

Host a party on a **boat** in the bay.

792- 九月／kugatsu [n] *September*

九月になって少し涼しくなってきた。
It has become a little cooler in **September**.

793- きっかけ／kikkake [n] *chance, occasion, opportunity*

友達のパーティがきっかけで彼に会った。
I had the **chance** to meet him at a friend's party.

794- 授業／jugyoo [n] *lesson, class*

この先生の歴史の授業はつまらない。
This teacher's history **class** is boring.

795- 亡くなる／nakunaru [v] *die, pass away*

近所のご老人が亡くなる。
An elderly man in our neighborhood **passed away**.

796- 止める／tomeru [v] *stop, turn off, park*

自然の資源節約のために水を止める。
Turn off the water to save natural resources.

797- 不思議／fushigi [na-adj] *wonderful, mysterious*

不思議な偶然が続く。
Mysterious coincidences continued to happen.

798- 茶／cha [n] *tea*

お茶は熱いうちがおいしい。
Tea is at its best when it's still hot.

799- 直接／chokusetsu [na-adj] *direct, firsthand*

わからないことは直接聞いた方がいい。
If you don't know you should ask **directly**.

110

800- バス/basu [n] *bus*

駅<ruby>駅<rt>えき</rt></ruby>までバスに<ruby>乗<rt>の</rt></ruby>る。

I take the **bus** to the station.

801- 効果/kooka [n] *effect*

<ruby>薬<rt>くすり</rt></ruby>の**効果**<ruby><rt>こうか</rt></ruby>が<ruby>現<rt>あらわ</rt></ruby>れるまで<ruby>二週間<rt>にしゅうかん</rt></ruby>かかる。

It will take two weeks for the medicine to have an **effect**.

802- 現実/genjitsu [n] *reality*

現実<ruby><rt>げんじつ</rt></ruby>は<ruby>理想<rt>りそう</rt></ruby>とは<ruby>違<rt>ちが</rt></ruby>う。

Reality can be different from expectation.

803- 触れる/fureru [v] *touch, experience*

<ruby>赤<rt>あか</rt></ruby>ちゃんの<ruby>肌<rt>はだ</rt></ruby>に**触**<ruby><rt>ふ</rt></ruby>**れる**。

Touch the baby's skin.

804- 飼う/kau [v] *raise, own (animal)*

<ruby>番犬<rt>ばんけん</rt></ruby>を**飼**<ruby><rt>か</rt></ruby>**う**。

I **own** a guard dog.

805- しゃべる/shaberu [v] *talk, chat*

クラシック<ruby>音楽<rt>おんがく</rt></ruby>のコンサートでは**しゃべる**ことは<ruby>禁<rt>きん</rt></ruby>じられている。

You are not allowed to **talk** during classical music concerts.

806- 国民/kokumin [n] *citizen*

<ruby>外務省<rt>がいむしょう</rt></ruby>は**国民**<ruby><rt>こくみん</rt></ruby>を<ruby>保護<rt>ほご</rt></ruby>しています。

The Ministry of Foreign Affairs aims to protect Japanese **citizens**.

807- さす/sasu [v] *shine, pour, put*

<ruby>朝日<rt>あさひ</rt></ruby>が<ruby>窓<rt>まど</rt></ruby>から**さす**。

The morning sun **shines** off the window.

808- やり方/yarikata [n] *method, way*

会社のやり方には納得いかない。

I don't get the **way** this company works.

809- ずいぶん/zuibun [adv] *considerably, surprisingly*

ずいぶん大きなくまのぬいぐるみだね。

What a **surprisingly** big stuffed bear.

810- 日本語/Nihongo [n] *Japanese (language)*

日本語にもいろいろな方言がある。

There are many dialects in **Japanese**.

811- 十月/juugatsu [n] *October*

十月にはハロウィーンがある。

We have Halloween in **October**.

812- 気分/kibun [n] *feeling, mood*

気分転換に散歩にいこう。

Let's take a walk for a change of **mood**.

813- 開発/kaihatsu [n] *development, exploitation*

都市開発が進行中です。

City **development** is well under way.

814- 殺す/korosu [v] *kill*

殺虫剤で虫を殺す。

Kill insects with pesticides.

815- 特徴/tokuchoo [n] *feature, trait*

新しいモデルの特徴はカメラです。

The special **feature** of the new model is the camera.

816- 神/kami [n] *god, divinity, spirit*

神社は神が祀られている場所だ。

A shrine is a place for **Gods.**

817- 暮らす/kurasu [v] *live*

田舎で暮らすのもいいことだ。

It's nice to **live** in the countryside.

818- 飛ぶ/tobu [v] *fly, jump*

ジェット機が高く飛ぶ。

Jet planes **fly** high in the sky.

819- 終わり/owari [n] *the end*

今日の授業はこれで終わりです。

This is **the end** of today's lesson.

820- 雑誌/zasshi [n] *journal, magazine*

金融雑誌を購読しています。

I subscribe to a financial **journal.**

821- 怒る/okoru [v] *get angry, scold*

父はすぐ怒る。

My father **gets angry** in an instant.

822- 整備/seebi [n] *maintenance, servicing*

車を整備に出す。

I need to take my car in for **maintenance.**

823- んと/nto [interj] *uh, huh, well*

んと、何だったっけ。

Uh, what was it?

824- 建物/tatemono [n] *building, structure*

ニューヨークは高い建物が多い。

There are a lot of high-rise **buildings** in New York City.

825- 発見/hakken [n] *discovery, detection*

科学の発見はおもしろい。

Scientific **discoveries** are interesting.

826- 相談/soodan [n] *consultation*

先生に相談する。

I had a **consultation** with my teacher.

827- 連絡/renraku [n] *contact, communication*

お客様リストに連絡先を入力する。

Enter **contact** information in the customer list.

828- 止まる/tomaru [v] *stop*

交差点に「止まれ」という標識がある。

There is a **stop** sign at the intersection.

829- 一生懸命/isshoo kenmee [na-adj] *with utmost effort*

何事も一生懸命がんばる。

Do your best at everything you try.

830- 用意/yooi [n] *preparation, arrangement*

プレゼンのための用意をする必要があります。

I need to **prepare** for the presentation.

831- 変/hen [na-adj] *strange, odd*

昨日の夜、変な夢を見た。

I had a **strange** dream last night.

832- 十二月/juunigatsu [n] *December*

十二月は年末の大掃除で忙しい。

December is busy with year-end cleaning.

833- 学ぶ/manabu [v] *learn, take lessons in*

料理教室で懐石料理を学ぶ。

I am **learning** *Kaiseki** cuisine at a cooking class.
*Tea ceremory dishes served in a course style.

834- 突然/totsuzen [adv] *suddenly*

突然、衝突音が聞こえました。

Suddenly, I heard a crashing sound.

835- 首/kubi [n] *neck*

きりんの首は長い。

Giraffes have long **necks**.

836- 設定/settee [n] *setting, setup, configuration*

新しいパソコンの設定を確認した。

I checked the **configuration** of my new computer.

837- ゆっくり/yukkuri [adv] *slowly, at ease*

ゆっくり深呼吸して落ち着く。

Breathe **slowly** and calm down.

838- 目指す/mezasu [v] *aim at, aim for*

山の頂上を目指す。

Aim at getting to the top of the mountain.

839- したがって/shitagatte [conj] *therefore, consequently*

したがって、この条例が承認されました。

Therefore, this regulation has been approved.

840- 一月/ichi gatsu [n] *January*

一月は一年の最初の月だ。

January is the first month of the year.

841- 成す/nasu [v] *build up, form, become, achieve*

目的を成す。

Achieve your goals.

842- 集める/atsumeru [v] *collect, assemble*

法律を変える署名を集める。

Collect signatures that are in favor of changing the law.

843- 失う/ushinau [v] *lose*

失うものより得るものの方が多い。

I will gain more than I **lose**.

844- 光/hikari [n] *light*

光がまぶしい。

The **light** is dazzling.

845- 並ぶ/narabu [v] *line up, stand in a line*

白線の内側に並ぶ。

Line up inside the white line.

846- 八月/hachi gatsu [n] *August*

八月のお盆に田舎に帰る。

I go back to my hometown for the Obon* festival in **August**.
*Annual lantern festival starting August 13th through 16th.

847- とく/toku [aux] *have it done*

それは最初にやっとくように。

116

You'd better **get it done** first.

848- 七月／shichi gatsu [n] *July*

七月にはたなばたがある。

There is the Tanabata* festival in **July**.

*Tanabata, also known as the Star Festival on July 7, involves a Japanese tradition in which people write their wishes on strips of paper and hang them on a bamboo tree.

849- 美しい／utsukushii [i-adj] *beautiful*

彼女の髪は美しい。

Her hair is **beautiful**.

850- 五月／go gatsu [n] *May*

五月はこどもの日にこいのぼりをかざる。

In **May**, we display flying carp for Children's Day.

851- 優しい／yasashii [i-adj] *tender, kind, gentle*

彼女は優しい人だ。

She is a **kind** person.

852- タバコ／tabako [n] *tobacco*

職場でタバコを吸ってはいけない。

Smoking **tobacco** is prohibited in the office.

853- 後ろ／ushiro [n] *back, behind*

後ろにも人がたくさん並んでいる。

There are a lot of people lining up **behind** me.

854- 六月／roku gatsu [n] *June*

六月は梅雨の時期です。

It's the rainy season in **June**.

855- 異なる/kotonaru [v] *differ, vary, be different*

父親が**異なる**弟がいます。

I have a brother who has a **different** father.

856- 十一月/juu ichi gatsu [n] *November*

十一月は秋の食べ物がおいしくなる。

Seasonal autumn food is especially good in **November**.

857- 新た/arata [na-adj] *new, fresh*

新しい仕事で、**新た**なスタートを切りましょう。

Get a **fresh** start with the new job.

858- 飛行機/hikooki [n] *airplane, aircraft*

飛行機で海外に行く。

Go abroad by **airplane**.

859- 至る/itaru [v] *arrive at, reach, get to*

会議でこの決定に**至る**。

The decision was **reached** at the meeting.

860- 午前/gozen[n] *morning, A.M.*

午前中に洗濯をすませる。

Finish the laundry in the **morning**.

861- 育てる/sodateru [v] *raise*

みどりがめを**育てる**。

I am **raising** a green turtle.

862- 種類/shurui [n] *variety, kind, category*

最近はいろいろな**種類**の携帯電話があります。

There is a wide **variety** of mobile phones nowadays.

863- 商品/shoohin [n] *goods, merchandise*

商品が宅配で届く。

The **merchandise** arrived by home delivery.

864- 生じる/shoojiru [v] *cause, produce*

二酸化炭素が生じる。

Carbon dioxide is **produced**.

865- イギリス/igirisu [n] *England (Great Britain, United Kingdom)*

フィッシュ＆チップスはイギリスの料理だ。

Fish and chips are a **British** food.

866- 大好き/daisuki [na-adj] *loveable, very likeable, favorite*

大好きなキャラクターの商品を買う。

I bought some of my **favorite** character's goods.

867- 語る/kataru [v] *talk about, narrate*

おじいさんが昔の話を語る。

My grandfather **talks about** old times.

868- 胸/mune [n] *chest, breast*

胸のレントゲンを撮った。

I had a **chest** x-ray.

869- 頼む/tanomu [v] *request, beg, order, ask for*

頼むから手伝ってほしい。

I am **asking for** your help.

870- 体験/taiken [n] *physical experience, personal experience*

キャンプで自然の体験をした。

I enjoyed a nature **experience** at the camp.

871- 材料/zairyoo [n] *ingredients, material*

料理の材料を買う。

I will go shopping for the **ingredients**.

872- 広がる/hirogaru [v] *spread, extend*

友達の輪が広がる。

My friendship circle is **spreading**.

873- きちんと/kichinto [adv] *precisely, neatly*

きちんと靴をそろえる。

Line up your shoes **neatly**.

874- そちら/sochira [pron] *there, that way*

そちらの商品を見せてください。

Please show me **that** product.

875- 勝つ/katsu [v] *win, gain victory*

決勝で勝つ。

Win the final.

876- 運動/undoo [n] *exercise, movement*

週に三回は運動したい。

I would like to **exercise** three times a week.

877- 捨てる/suteru [v] *throw away, abandon*

いらないものを捨てる。

Throw away things you don't need.

878- 幸せ/shiawase [n] *happiness, luck*

幸せは自分が感じるものです。

Happiness is inside you.

879- 通す/toosu [v] *pass, stick through*

針に糸を通す。

Put the thread **through** the needle.

880- 横/yoko [n] *side, beside*

コーヒーの横に砂糖を置く。

Put the sugar **next to** the coffee.

881- 伴う/tomonau [v] *accompany, go/come together*

この冒険には危険が伴う。

This adventure **comes with** some danger

882- 命/inochi [n] *life*

子供に命の大切さを教える。

Teach children the importance of **life**.

883- 流れ/nagare [n] *stream, current*

川の流れが早くなる。

The **current** of the river is getting faster.

884- 育つ/sodatsu [v] *be raised, grow up*

子供が育つのは早い。

Children **grow up** fast.

885- 予定/yotee [n] *plans, schedule*

明日の予定を確認する。

Confirm tomorrow's **schedule**.

121

886- ちなみに/chinamini [conj] *by the way, incidentally*

ちなみに、この町の名前は昔の武士の名前です。

By the way, this town is named after an old samurai.

887- 決して/kesshite [adv] *never, by no means*

決して人の悪口を言わない。

Never say bad things about people.

888- 馬/uma [n] *horse*

白い馬に乗った王子様に会いたい。

I wish to meet a prince riding on a white **horse**.

889- 完全/kanzen [na-adj] *perfect, complete*

まだ完全でない。

It's not **perfect** yet.

890- 学生/gakusee [n] *student*

この町は大学生でいっぱいだ。

This town is full of college **student**s.

891- 性格/seekaku [n] *character, personality*

人の性格と血液型の関係を信じる人もいる。

Some people believe in a link between a person's blood type and their **personality**.

892- 死/shi [n] *death*

死はだれにも訪れるものだ。

Death comes to us all.

893- 位置/ichi [n] *place, location*

今いる**位置**を地図で確認する。

Check our current **location** on the map.

894- 発展/hatten [n] *development, expansion*

20世紀の技術の**発展**は すごい。

Technological **development** in the 20th century has been amazing.

895- おかしい/okashii [i-adj] *funny, strange*

彼は**おかしい**話をするのが上手だ。

He is good at telling **funny** stories.

896- 近所/kinjo [n] *neighborhood*

近所のコンビニに行く。

I am going to a convenience store in the **neighborhood**.

897- 一本/ippon [n] *one (cylindrical object)*

一本の大きな大根がとれた。

I managed to get **one** big daikon.

898- 張る/haru [v] *stretch, put up*

庭に洗濯のロープを**張る**。

I will **put up** a laundry rope in the backyard.

899- ご飯/gohan [n] *cooked rice, meal*

炊きたての**ご飯**がおいしい。

Freshly cooked **rice** is delicious.

900- 危険/kiken [n] *danger, risk*

雪崩の**危険**がある。

There is a **risk** of an avalanche.

901- かしら/kashira [p] *wondering*

今日は雨が降るの**かしら**。
I **wonder** if it's going to rain today.

902- すなわち/sunawachi [conj] *that is, namely*

リンガ・フランカとは、**すなわち**共通の言語のことです。
That is to say, Lingua Franca is the common language.

903- 海外/kaigai [n] *foreign, abroad, overseas*

海外に行くので英会話を習う。
I am learning English conversation because I am going **abroad**.

904- 教育/kyooiku [n] *education, training*

教育の格差は国の問題だ。
Disparity in **education** is a national issue.

905- 想像/soozoo [n] *imagination, guess*

子供は**想像**力でいっぱいだ。
Children are full of **imagination**.

906- 実は/jitsuwa [adv]*as a matter of fact, to tell you the truth*

実は、ビザの期限がもうすぐ切れます。
To tell you the truth, my visa is about to expire.

907- 許す/yurusu [v] *permit, allow, forgive*

子供のいたずらを**許す**。
Forgive the children for their mischief.

908- 表/hyoo [n] *table, chart*

データは**表**にするとわかりやすい。
The data is easy to understand when shown in **table**.

909- 文化/bunka [n] *culture, civilization*

それぞれの国の文化はすばらしい。

Each country has a wonderful **culture**.

910- 八/hachi [num] *eight*

日本の迷信では、八は縁起のいい数字です。

According to a Japanese superstition, the number **eight** a lucky number.

911- 食べ物/tabemono [n] *food*

食べ物を無駄にしない。

Don't waste **food**.

912- 借りる/ kariru [v] *borrow, rent*

図書館で本を借りる。

I **am borrowing** some books from the library.

913- だけれど/da-keredo [cp] *though, despite*

とても行きたいのだけれど、パーティに行けない。

I can't go to the party, **though** I really would love to.

914- 準備/junbi [n] *preparation, setup*

一日でコンサートの準備をする。

We'll do the **setup** for the concert in one day.

915- 二月/ni gatsu [n] *February*

二月の節分に豆まきをしよう。

You throw beans for the Setsubun* festival in **February**.

*Spring festival held on the day of seasonal division between winter and spring.

916- 月/tsuki [n] *moon, month*

月の裏側を見てみたい。

I wish I could see the other side of the **moon**.

917- 世の中/yo no naka [n] *society, the world*

世の中は暗いニュースが多い。

There is a lot of depressing news in **the world**.

918- インターネット/intaanetto [n] *Internet*

インターネットは検索に便利だ。

The **Internet** is useful for research.

919- 春/haru [n] *spring*

春は始まりの季節なので好きだ。

I like **spring** as it is the time for a new beginning.

920- 旅/tabi [n] *travel, journey*

たまには一人で旅にいくのもよい。

Sometimes, it's good to go on a **trip** alone.

921- 二年/ninen [n] *two years*

日本語を習い始めてから二年になります。

It's been **two years** since I started learning Japanese.

922- 寒い/samui [i-adj] *cold*

東北地方の冬は寒い。

The Tohoku region has very **cold** winters.

923- 同様/dooyoo [n] *identical, same, similarity*

正社員と同様の仕事をする。

I am doing the **same** tasks as full-time employees.

924- 一般/ippan [n] *general, ordinary*

一般の入場はおことわりします。

We are not open for **general** admission.

925- 第一/daiichi [n] *foremost*

第一に安全を考えよう。

Pay **foremost** attention to safety.

926- 三年/sannen [n] *three years*

日本の高校は三年間だ。

The high school curriculum in Japan is for **three years**.

927- 申す/mousu [v] *say, be called (humble)*

私は田中と申します。

I **am called** Tanaka.

928- 押す/osu [v] *push, press*

エレベーターで「閉まる」のボタンを押す。

Push the close button in the elevator.

929- 責任/sekinin [n] *duty, responsibility*

マネージャーが責任をとる。

The manager will take **responsibility**.

930- 選択/sentaku [n] *selection, choice, option*

算数は選択問題の方が好きだ。

I prefer multiple **choice** questions in math.

931- 負ける/makeru [v] *lose, defeated*

野球の試合で負ける。

We might **lose** the baseball game.

932- 技術/gijutsu [n] *technology, engineering*

医療の技術がどんどん進む。

Medical **technology** is advancing rapidly.

933- 一般的/ippanteki [na-adj] *popular, typical, general*

一般的な意見に従う。

Stay in line with **popular** opinion.

934- そば/soba [n] *near, close*

そばにいなさい。

Stay **close** to me.

935- 減る/heru [v] *decrease, diminish , decline*

日本の人口が減る。

The Japanese population is **declining**.

936- 記事/kiji [n] *article, report*

芸能人同士の結婚の記事を目にした。

I saw an **article** about marriages between celebrities.

937- 本人/honnin [n] *the person himself*

生年月日で本人確認をする。

Confirm **his own** identity by checking his date of birth.

938- 焼く/yaku [v] *burn, roast, grill*

庭で肉を焼く。

Grill meat in the backyard.

939- たまに/tamani [adv] *occasionally*

たまにホームパーティをします。

Occasionally, I hold a home party.

940- 慣れる/nareru [v] *get used to*

一年が過ぎて仕事に慣れる。

I am **getting used to** my job after a year.

941- もしくは/moshikuwa [conj] *or, otherwise*

電話もしくはメールでお問い合わせください。

Please contact us by phone **or** email.

942- 出会う/deau [v] *meet, come across*

彼とネットで出会った。

I **met** him on the Internet.

943- 推進/suishin [n] *drive, promotion*

町おこしを推進する。

Promote the revival of the town.

944- 自ら/mizukara [n] *oneself, personally, own*

自ら子ども食堂を始める。

I am going to **personally** start a Children's Cafeteria*.

*Children's Cafeteria provides meals for children in poverty for free or at low cost by using ingredients donated by supporters.

945- 作業/ sagyoo [n] *work, operation, duty, task*

面倒な作業は先延ばしにしよう。

Let's leave the complicated **task** for later.

946- 私自身/watashi-jishin [pron] *myself, my own*

私自身の体験をお話しします。

I would like to talk about **my own** experience.

129

947- たび/tabi [n] *time, times*

上司（じょうし）に会（あ）うたびに叱（しか）られる。

Every **time** I meet with my boss, I get scolded.

948- 付き合う/tsukiau [v] *go out with, go along with, associate with*

彼（かれ）と付（つ）き合（あ）う。

I am **going out with** him.

949- 半分/hanbun [n] *half*

ケーキを半分（はんぶん）に切（き）る。

Cut the cake in **half**.

950- 条件/jooken [n] *condition, term*

いい条件（じょうけん）の仕事（しごと）が見（み）つからない。

I have not found a job with good **conditions**.

951- 医者/isha [n] *doctor, physician*

医者（いしゃ）も病気（びょうき）になる。

Doctors can get sick as well.

952- 振る/furu [v] *wave, swing, sprinkle*

ゴルフのクラブを振（ふ）る。

Swing the gold club.

953- 関心/kanshin [n] *concern, interest*

世間（せけん）の関心（かんしん）の高（たか）いニュースを読（よ）む。

Read news articles that have a strong public **interest**.

954- 表示/hyooji [n] *indication, display*

車で地図の画面を表示する。

Display a map on the screen in the car.

955- 秋/aki [n] *autumn, fall*

秋は紅葉がきれいだ。

It's beautiful when the leaves change color in the **fall**.

956- 明るい/akarui [i-adj] *bright, cheerful*

この部屋は日当たりがいいので明るい。

This room is **bright** with plenty of sunlight.

957- 趣味/shumi [n] *hobby, tastes*

私の趣味はキルトです。

My **hobby** is quilting.

958- 生徒/seeto [n] *pupil, student*

今週は先生が生徒の家を訪問する。

Teachers will visit **pupils'** homes this week.

959- 相当/sootoo [adv] *considerably, pretty*

忙しいので相当疲れがたまっている。

I have been very busy, so I am feeling **pretty** tired.

960- 従う/shitagau [v] *abide by, obey, follow*

会社のルールに従う。

I **abide by** the company's rules.

961- 検討(する)/kentoo (suru) [v] *consider, discuss, examine*

新しいルールについて検討する。

We will **consider** the new rule.

962- 占める/shimeru [v] *occupy, account for*

高齢者は日本の人口の四分の一以上を**占める**。

Elderly people **account for** more than a quarter of the Japanese population.

963- まさに/masani [adv] *exactly, certainly*

まさに夢で見た通りになる。

What I saw in my dream is **exactly** happening.

964- 選手/senshu [n] *player, team member*

水泳の**選手**に選れる。

I am going to be selected as a **member** of the swim team.

965- 以下/ika [n] *not exceeding, and under*

三歳**以下**は入場できない。

No admission for those three-years of age **and under**.

966- 大きさ/ookisa [n] *size, dimensions*

電池の**大きさ**が違う。

The battery **sizes** are different.

967- 調査/choosa [n] *investigation, survey*

顧客**調査**を行う。

We are conducting a customer **survey**.

968- 分/bun [n] *segment, share*

みんなの**分**をお皿に分ける。

Put everyone's **share** on their plates.

969- 実家/jikka [n] *(one's parents') home*

お正月に実家に帰る。

We visit **our parents' home** for the New Year holiday.

970- 発表/happyoo [n] *announcement, presentation*

新しい携帯電話のモデルが発表された。

The new mobile phone model was **announced**.

971- むしろ/mushiro [adv] *rather, better*

私はむしろ、前の案の方がいいと思います。

I **rather** think the previous plan is better.

972- 作成/sakusee [n] *creating, writing, draw up*

講演の原稿を作成する。

We will **draw up** a draft for the lecture.

973- 名/na [n] *name, given name*

新しく発見された星に名をつける。

Give a **name** to the newly found star.

974- 確保(する)/kakuho (suru) [v] *guarantee, secure*

必要な食料を確保する。

Secure the necessary food.

975- まるで/marude [adv] *quite, as if, just like*

まるで夢のような話だ。

It is **just like** a dream.

976- 運ぶ/hakobu [v] *carry, transport*

お皿をテーブルに運ぶ。

Carry the plates to the table.

977- こともある/kotomo-aru [cp] *sometimes happens*

思い通りにならない**こともある**。

Sometimes, things do not go as planned.

978- ちゃいけない/cha-ikenai [cp] *must not*

授業中はおしゃべりし**ちゃいけない**。

You **must not** chat during the lesson.

979- てはいけない/tewa-ikenai [cp] *must not*

教室の中で走っ**てはいけない**。

You **must not** run in the classroom.

980- 正しい/tadashii [i-adj] *right, accurate*

先生の言うことが**正しい**とは限らない。

Teachers are not always **right**.

981- ほぼ/hobo [adv] *about, nearly, almost*

数字は**ほぼ**合っています。

The numbers are **almost** correct.

982- 表わす/arawasu [v] *show, express*

謝罪を文書で**表わす**。

Express an apology in writing.

983- 毎年/maitoshi [n] *every year, annual*

毎年、運動会が行われる。

The field athletics day is held **every year**.

984- 文字/moji [n] *letter, character*

文字ばけして読めない。

The **characters** are garbled and illegible.

985- 空/sora [n] *sky*

空に飛行機が見える。

I see an airplane up in the **sky**.

986- に対し/ni-taishi [cp] *toward, against*

店に対し苦情を言う。

Make a complaint **against** the store.

987- 明日/ashita [n] *tomorrow*

明日までの締め切りの仕事がある。

I have an assignment due **tomorrow**.

988- 役割/yakuwari [n] *part, role*

自分の役割を果たす。

Perform your own **role**.

989- 地球/chikyuu [n] *earth, globe*

地球は平らだと思われていた。

People used to think the **earth** was flat.

990- 公園/kooen [n] *park*

公園のベンチで休む。

Rest on a bench in the **park**.

991- 個人/kojin [n] *individual, personal*

個人情報のセキュリティを強化する。

Enhance the security of **personal** information.

992- やら/yara [p] *and, or*

子供たちがハロウィーンでキャンディやらチョコレートやらをもらった。

Children got candies **and** chocolate on Halloween.

993- 消える/kieru [v] *go off, disappear*

停電で明かりが消える。

The lights will **go off** when there is a power failure.

994- 激しい/hageshii [i-adj] *fierce, intense*

台風で激しい雨が降る。

We get **intense** rain when there is a typhoon.

995- 短い/mijikai [i-adj] *short*

短い文の方がわかりやすい。

Short sentences are easier to understand.

996- 薬/kusuri [n] *medicine*

アトピーにいい薬が見つかった。

We found a good **medication** for skin allergies.

997- 試合/shiai [n] *game, match*

野球の試合を見に行く。

We are going to see a baseball **game**.

998- 成長/seichoo [n] *growth*

子供の成長が楽しみだ。

I'm looking forward to the **growth** of my child.

999- おなか/onaka [n] *stomach, belly*

父のおなかは出ている。

My father's **belly** is sticking out.

1000- 機能/kinoo [n] *function, capability*

高い機能のタブレットを持っている。

I have a tablet with high-level **functionality**.

1001- ボール/booru [n] *ball*

ボールで遊んではいけない公園がある。

Some playgrounds do not allow you to play with **balls**.

1002- 少年/shoonen [n] *boy, juvenile*

彼らはボーイスカウトの少年たちだ。

Those **boys** are in the Boy Scouts.

1003- 方向/hookoo [n] *direction*

方向がわからなくなってしまった。

I lost my sense of **direction**.

1004- 遅い/osoi [i-adj] *late, slow*

今朝は遅いスタートだ。

We have a **late** start this morning.

1005- 資料/shiryoo [n] *document, material*

大事な資料を失くして怒られる。

I will get in trouble for losing this important **document**.

1006- タイプ/taipu [n] *type*

彼女は僕の好みのタイプではない。

She is not my **type**.

1007- 扱う/atsukau [v] *deal with, handle*

割れ物は丁寧に扱う。

We should **handle** fragile items with care.

1008- 指摘/shiteki (suru) [v] *point out, indicate*

間違いを指摘する。

Point out any errors.

1009- ヨーロッパ/yooroppa [n] *Europe*

ヨーロッパは人気の旅行先です。

Europe is a popular travel destination.

1010- 除く/nozoku [v] *remove, get rid of*

虫歯を治療で取り**除く**。

Cavities can be **removed** by the dentist.

1011- それら/sorera [pron] *those, these, they*

それらはセール商品です。

Those are on sale.

1012- ご存知/go-zonji [n] *knowing (honorific)*

はやりの特殊詐欺について**ご存知**ですか。

Do you **know** about a particular fraud that is going around?

1013- 意外/igai [na-adj] *unexpected, surprising*

意外な事実がわかった。

A **surprising** fact has been revealed.

1014- 一週間/isshuukan [n] *one week*

出張から**一週間**で戻ります。

I will return from a business trip in **one week**.

1015- 何回/nan-kai [n] *how many times?*

パスワードは**何回**まで入力できますか。

How many times can I enter my password?

1016- 政府/seefu [n] *government*

これは**政府**が後援する事業です。

This is a **government**-sponsored project.

138

1017- 分ける/wakeru [v] *divide, classify*

生徒をレベルで分ける。

Divide students by level.

1018- 計画/keekaku [n] *plan, schedule*

計画通りに進んでいます。

It is going according to **plan**.

1019- 段階/dankai [n] *stage, phase*

これはまだ計画段階です。

This is still in the planning **stage**.

1020- 量/ryoo [n] *quantity, volume, amount*

量よりも質が大事です。

Quality is more important than **quantity**.

1021- 田舎/inaka [n] *countryside, one's hometown*

田舎に引退したいと思います。

I would like to retire to the **countryside**.

1022- 感動(する)/kandou (suru) [v] *be impressed, be moved*

パラリンピックに感動した。

I **was moved** by the Paralympics.

1023- スポーツ/supootsu [n] *sport*

健康のためにスポーツをするべきだ。

I should play some **sports** for my health.

1024- 感覚/kankaku [n] *sense, feeling*

寒さで指の感覚がなくなった。

I have no **feeling** in my fingers.

1025- 地元/jimoto [n] *local, local area*

地元の人気のレストランに行きたい。

I want to go to a popular **local** restaurant.

1026- 勝手/katte [na-adj] *at one's convenience, on one's own, without consulting*

妻が勝手に高い物を買った。

My wife went out and made a large purchase **without consulting** me.

1027- さすが /sasuga [adv] *as one would expect*

さすが彼はリーダーシップがある。

As one would expect, he has leadership abilities.

1028- 寂しい/sabishii [i-adj] *lonely, lonesome*

一人暮らしは寂しい。

I feel **lonely** living alone.

1029- 再び/futatabi [adv] *again, once more*

再び挑戦したい。

I want to try it **again.**

1030- 利く/kiku [v] *act, work, be effective*

この薬はよく効く。

This medicine **works** well.

1031- 勤める/tsutomeru [v] *be employed, work for*

金融企業に勤める。

I **work for** a financial company.

1032- 吸う/suu [v] *breathe in, smoke*

私 は昼休みにビルの外でたばこを吸う。

I **smoke** outside the building during the lunch break.

1033- 流す/nagasu [v] *flush, drain*

トイレを流す。

Flush the toilet.

1034- 希望/kiboo [n] *hope, wish*

希望を持ち続けています。

I continue to have **hope**.

1035- 急/kyuu [na-adj] *urgent, sudden, steep*

急な坂で滑った。

I slipped on a **steep** hill.

1036- 勧める/susumeru [v] *encourage, recommend*

友達に健康食品を勧める。

I **recommend** health food to my friends.

1037- 年齢/nenree [n] *age, years*

彼女は年齢より若く見える。

She looks younger than her **age**.

1038- フランス/furansu [n] *France*

フランスのパリに行ってみたい。

I want to visit Paris, in **France**.

1039- 仕方/shikata [n] *method, way, how to*

車の運転の仕方を知りません。

I don't know **how to** drive a car.

1040- なし/nashi [n] *without, no*

砂糖<ruby>砂糖<rt>さとう</rt></ruby>なしでクッキーを<ruby>作<rt>つく</rt></ruby>る。

Make cookies **without** sugar.

1041- さて/sate [conj] *now, well*

さて、<ruby>次<rt>つぎ</rt></ruby>の<ruby>話題<rt>わだい</rt></ruby>に<ruby>移<rt>うつ</rt></ruby>りましょう。

Now, let's move onto the next topic.

1042- 疲れる/tsukareru [v] *get tired*

トリックオアトリートで<ruby>歩<rt>ある</rt></ruby>き<ruby>回<rt>まわ</rt></ruby>るのは<ruby>疲<rt>つか</rt></ruby>れる。

I **get tired** from walking around for trick or treating.

1043- 落とす/otosu [v] *drop, lose*

バッグを<ruby>線路<rt>せんろ</rt></ruby>に<ruby>落<rt>お</rt></ruby>とす。

I **drop** my bag on the track.

1044- 人気/ninki [n] *popularity*

アイドルにとって<ruby>人気<rt>にんき</rt></ruby>は<ruby>大事<rt>だいじ</rt></ruby>だ。

Popularity is important for idols.

1045- 弱い/yowai [i-adj] *weak*

<ruby>弱<rt>よわ</rt></ruby>い<ruby>者<rt>もの</rt></ruby>をいじめるのは<ruby>恥<rt>は</rt></ruby>ずかしいことだ。

It is nothing but an embarrassment to bully the **weak**.

1046- まとめる/matomeru [v] *summarize, settle*

みんなの<ruby>意見<rt>いけん</rt></ruby>をまとめる。

Summarize everyone's opinions.

1047- 格好/kakkoo [n] *appearance, look*

<ruby>彼<rt>かれ</rt></ruby>は<ruby>人々<rt>ひとびと</rt></ruby>をおかしい<ruby>格好<rt>かっこう</rt></ruby>で<ruby>笑<rt>わら</rt></ruby>わせました。

He made people laugh with his funny **appearance**.

1048- 渡る/wataru [v] *cross, go across*

青信号で交差点を渡る。

We **cross** the intersection on the green light.

1049- 患者/kanja [n] *patient*

多くの患者が医者のオフィスで待っています。

There are many **patients** waiting at the doctor's office.

1050- 壁/kabe [n] *wall, barrier*

壁登りは人気のあるアトラクションです。

Wall climbing is a popular attraction.

1051- 道路/dooro [n] *road, street*

その道路は工事中です。

The **road** is under construction.

1052- 参る*/mairu [v] *go, come (humble)*

ご挨拶に参ります。

I will **go** to pass on my greetings.

*The phrase "mairu" is usually used in its extended polite form of "mairimasu".

1053- 反対/hantai [n] *opposite*

そのキャンペーンには私は反対の立場です。

I am taking an **opposing** position to the campaign.

1054- 他人/tanin [n] *stranger, others*

他人と話をしないように。

Do not talk to **strangers**.

1055- 提供/teekyoo (suru) [v] *offer, sponsor*

その番組は我が社が提供しています。

Our company **sponsors** that program.

1056- 空気/kuuki [n] *air, atmosphere*

この辺りは空気の質が悪い。

The **air** quality is poor in this area.

1057- 去年/kyonen [n] *last year*

この服は去年買いました。

I bought these clothes **last year**.

1058- 肩/kata [n] *shoulder*

長い時間タイプしていたので肩が凝っています。

My **shoulders** are stiff from typing for such a long time.

1059- 知れる/shireru [v] *come to light, be known, be able to know*

結末を知れるのは映画を見た人だけです。

The only way to **be able to know** the end of the movie is to watch it.

1060- 匂い/nioi [n] *smell, odor*

キッチンで変な匂いがする。

There is a strange **odor** in the kitchen.

1061- 銀行/ginkoo [n] *bank*

銀行で送金をした。

I transferred some funds at the **bank**.

1062- 実現(する)/jitsugen (suru) [v] *realize, come true*

夢を**実現**する。

My dream will **come true**.

1063- ありがとう/arigatoo [interj] *Thank you.*

教えてくれて**ありがとう**。

Thank you for letting me know.

1064- 購入/koonyuu [n] *purchase*

家を**購入**する。

We are **purchasing** a house.

1065- 十年/juu-nen [n] *ten years*

十年前に日本に来ました。

I came to Japan **ten years** ago.

1066- 右/migi [n] *right*

右を見て、左を見て、**右**を見てから道を渡る。

Look **right**, look left, then look **right again** before crossing the street.

1067- 全体/zentai [n] *entire, whole, overall*

全体のバランスを考える。

Consider the **overall** balance.

1068- 認識/ninshiki (suru) [v] *recognize, be aware*

人口知能はすべての方言を**認識**できない。

Artificial intelligence cannot **recognize** every dialect.

1069- 安心/anshin [n] *peace of mind, relief*

安心のために、ゲート付きのマンションに住む。

I live in a gated apartment for **peace of mind**.

1070- 雪/yuki [n] *snow*

さっぽろ雪祭りに行きます。

We are going to the Sapporo **Snow** Festival*.

*A large snow and ice sculpture exhibit held annually in Hokkaido.

1071- ポイント/pointo [n] *point (score)*

店のカードのポイントを集める。

Collect **points** on store cards.

1072- 十/juu [num] *ten*

かくれんぼで十まで数える。

Count to **ten** when playing hide and seek.

1073- 仲間/nakama [n] *company, fellow, mate*

クラブの仲間と旅行に行く。

Go on a trip with club **mates**.

1074- かつ/katsu [conj] *and, moreover, also*

能力かつ経験のある人材が求められている。

There is a demand for people with skills **and** experience.

1075- 知識/chishiki [n] *knowledge, information*

彼はワインの知識がある。

He has a good **knowledge** of wine.

1076- 多少/tashoo [adv] *more or less, somewhat*

それは多少思っていたのと違います。

That is **somewhat** different from what I thought.

1077- 緑/midori [n] *green*

信号は緑色なのに青信号と呼ばれます。

Although the traffic light is **green**, it is called a blue signal.

1078- 解決/kaiketsu [n] *solution, settlement*

この問題は**解決**するのに時間が必要だ。

This problem will take time to **solve**.

1079- 狭い/semai [i-adj] *narrow, tight*

狭い廊下に物を置かないでください。

Do not place objects in the **narrow** corridor.

1080- 一時間/ichi-jikan [n] one hour

これは**一時間**のプログラムです。

This is a one-hour program.

1081- 失敗/shippai [n] *failure, mistake*

失敗は成功のもとと言う。

It is said that **failure** is the source of success.

1082- いきなり/ikinari [adv] *suddenly, without notice*

いきなり声をかけられてびっくりした。

I was surprised when I **suddenly** heard a voice.

1083- 成功/seekoo [n] *success, achievement*

彼が科学の研究で**成功**することを祈る。

I wish him **success** in his scientific research.

1084- マンション/manshon [n] *condominium, high-rise apartment*

マンションの上の階に住みたい。

I want to live at the top of a **high-rise apartment** building.

1085- 協力/kyooryoku [n] *cooperation*

調査へのご**協力**、ありがとうございます。

Thank you for your **cooperation** with our survey.

1086- 伯父、叔父/oji [n] *uncle*

伯父は大きな車を持っています。

My **uncle** has a big car.

1087- 時々/tokidoki [adv] *sometimes*

時々絵を描きます。

I paint **sometimes**.

1088- 生む/umu [v] *produce, give birth*

事業から利益を生む。

Produce a profit from a business project.

1089- 産む/umu [v] *give birth*

子供を自宅で産む。

Give birth to a child at home.

1090- 卒業/sotsugyoo [n] *graduation*

春は卒業のシーズンだ。

Spring is the season for **graduation**s.

1091- 降る/furu [v] *fall, come down*

雪が降る。

Snow is going to **fall**.

1092- 野菜/yasai [n] *vegetable*

生の野菜が体にいい。

Raw **vegetables** are good for you.

1093- 自分自身/jibunjishin [pron] *oneself*

自分自身を大切にしなさい。

Look after **yourself**.

1094- 報告/hookoku [n] *report*

上司に**報告**をする。

Submit a **report** to your boss.

1095- 落ち着く/ochitsuku [v] *settle, calm down*

クラシックを聴くと気持ちが**落ち着く**。

Classical music helps me to **calm down**.

1096- 決定/kettei [n] *decision*

会議で方針が**決定**された。

A **decision** was made in the meeting to adopt the policy.

1097- 割合/wariai [n] *ratio, percentage*

スープの水の**割合**を増やす。

Increase the **ratio** of water in the soup.

1098- 移動/idoo [n] *movement, transfer, transport*

車で**移動**する。

Transport by car.

1099- いまだ /imada [adv] *still, yet, so far*

いまだに独身だ。

I am **still** single.

1100- 血/chi [n] *blood*

ころんで膝から**血**が出た。

I fell and got **blood** on my knees.

1101- 応じる/oojiru [v] *respond*

リクエストに**応じる**。

Respond to a request.

149

1102- 涙/namida [n] *tear*

目から涙が流れる。
Tears fall from their eyes.

1103- 表情/hyoojoo [n] *facial expression*

赤ちゃんがかわいい表情をしている。
Babies make adorable **facial expressions**.

1104- ああ/aa [adv] *like that*

ああいうのが好きです。
I like things **like that**.

1105- 逃げる/nigeru [n] *run away, escape*

火事から逃げる。
Run away from the fire.

1106- 次第/shidai [adv] *depend on, as soon as*

わかり次第お知らせします。
I will let you know **as soon as** we find out.

1107- 楽/raku [na-adj] *comfort, ease*

この椅子は楽だ。
This is a **comfortable** chair.

1108- やがて/yagate [adv] *soon, before long*

やがて彼女の意識が薄れていった。
She **soon** became unconscious.

1109- ではありません/dewa-arimasen [cp] *is/are not*

私は日本人ではありません。
I **am not** Japanese.

1110- じゃありません/ja-arimasen [cp] *is/are not*

それは好きじゃありません。
That **is not** my favorite.

1111- かつて/katsute [adv] *once before, a long time ago*

かつてこの辺りは野原だった。
Long ago, this area used to be a field.

1112- ごみ/gomi [n] *garbage, trash*

ごみは指定の場所に捨ててください。
Please leave **garbage** at the designated place.

1113- 警察/keisatsu [n] *police*

警察に電話する。
I call the **police**.

1114- 兄/ani [n] *elder brother*

三歳ちがいの兄がいます。
I have a **brother** three years **older** than me.

1115- 代わり/kawari [n] *substitute*

今日は代わりの先生が来た。
A **substitute** teacher came today.

1116- 外国/gaikoku [n] *foreign country, foreign*

外国のチーズを食べた。
I ate some **foreign** cheese.

1117- 細かい/komakai [i-adj] *small, fine, detailed*

細かいジグソーパズルに挑戦する。
I am working on a **detailed** jigsaw puzzle.

1118- 静か/shizuka [na-adj] *quiet, silent*

電車の中では**静か**にしてください。

Please be **quiet** on the train.

1119- 腰/koshi [n] *lower back, hip*

引っ越しで**腰**をいためた。

I hurt my **lower back** while moving.

1120- 開催/kaisai (suru) [v] *hold, open, host*

ボートレースが**開催**される。

A boat race is going to be **held**.

1121- 瞬間/shunkan [n] *moment*

会った**瞬間**に運命を感じた。

We sensed our destiny the **moment** we met.

1122- 近付く/chikazuku [v] *approach, get closer to*

犬に**近付く**。

Get closer to the dog.

1123- わずか/wazuka [na-adj] *a few, a little, only*

彼が**わずか**な希望だ。

He is our **only** hope.

1124- 暗い/kurai [i-adj] *dark, depressed*

暗い道では、気をつけてね。

Be careful on **dark** streets.

1125- 届く/todoku [v] *reach, arrive*

空に手が**届く**。

Reaching for the sky.

1126- 窓/mado [n] *window*

朝は窓をあけて空気を変えよう。

Open the **windows** in the morning and let in some fresh air.

1127- ストレス/sutoresu [n] *stress*

仕事のストレスがあります。

I have **stress** from work.

1128- 伸ばす/nobasu [v] *extend, stretch*

ジムで体を伸ばす。

I **stretch** my body at the gym.

1129- ドア/doa [n] *door*

ドアは静かに閉めましょう。

Please close the **door** quietly.

1130- 森/mori [n] *woods, forest*

森の中の小屋で暮らしてみたい。

I want to live in a cottage in the **woods**.

1131- 目標/mokuhyoo [n] *goal, target*

新年の目標を立てる。

Set a **goal** for the new year.

1132- 本来/honrai [adv] *originally, by nature*

その映画は本来子ども向けの小説でした。

The movie was **originally** written as a novel for children.

1133- 重い/omoi [i-adj] *heavy*

荷物が重い。

My bag is **heavy**.

1134- 変更/henkoo [n] *change, revision*

計画を変更する必要がある。。

We need to make a **revision** to the plan.

1135- 感謝/kansha [n] *appreciation, gratitude*

感謝の気持ちを込めて贈り物を送る。

Send a gift with **gratitude**.

1136- 腕/ude [n] *arm, skill*

ゴルフの腕があがった。

My golf **skills** have improved.

1137- 手術/shujutsu [n] *surgery, operation*

膝の手術を受ける。

I am having knee **surgery**.

1138- 当たり前/atarimae [na-adj] *usual, common, ordinary, accepted*

困っている人を助けるのは当たり前です。

Helping someone in trouble is just the **accepted** thing to do.

1139- 時点/jiten [n] *point in time*

今の時点では、結果はわからない。

We can't predict the outcome at this **point of time**.

1140- 馬鹿/baka [n] *fool*

馬と鹿を間違えた人のことを馬鹿と言っていたそうだ。

Apparently, calling someone a **fool*** is to say they can't tell a deer from a horse.

*The kanji characters for the word "baka" are "ba", which means horse, and "ka", which means deer.

1141- 忙しい/isogashii [i-adj] *busy, occupied*

今日はたくさんのお客様で忙しい。
It's **busy** with a lot of customers today.

1142- 愛する/aisuru [v] *love, care*

私は自分の家族を愛する。
I **love** my family.

1143- それでは/soredewa [conj] *then, now, so*

それでは、このようにしましょう。
So, let's do it this way.

1144- それじゃ/sorejaa [conj] *then, well, so*

それじゃ、また会いましょう。
Well, let's meet again.

1145- 遠い/tooi [i-adj] *far, distant*

動物園は駅から遠い。
The zoo is **far** from the station.

1146- 苦労/kuroo [n] *hardship, difficulty*

父は苦労した。
My father had some **difficulty**.

1147- 押さえる/osaeru [v] *press down, hold*

傷口を押さえる。
Press down on the wound.

1148- 課題/kadai [n] *assignment, task*

論文の課題がある。
I have an **assignment** to write an essay.

155

1149- とともに/to-tomoni [cp] *together with, along with*

子供_{こども}とともに親_{おや}も成長_{せいちょう}する。

Parents grow **along with** their children.

1150- 見つかる/mitsukaru [v] *be found, be discovered*

なくした宝物_{たからもの}が見_みつかる。

Lost treasures **are found**.

1151- うそ/uso [n] *lie*

うそ発見器_{はっけんき}を試_{ため}す。

Try out a **lie** detector.

1152- 仰る/ossharu [v] *say, tell, speak (honorific)*

先生_{せんせい}の仰_{おっしゃ}ることをきく。

Listen to what your teacher **says**.

1153- 主張/shuchoo [n] *argument, claim*

私_{わたし}の主張_{しゅちょう}が認_{みと}められました。

My **claim** was acknowledged.

1154- 施設/shisetsu [n] *institution, facility*

新_{あたら}しい子供向_{こどもむ}けの施設_{しせつ}に行_いく。

We are visiting the new **facility** for children.

1155- チェック/chekku [n] *check*

進捗状況_{しんちょくじょうきょう}をチェックする。

Check up on progress.

1156- 1ヶ月/ikkagetsu [n] *one month*

1ヶ月_{かげつ}の長_{なが}い旅行_{りょこう}に行_いく。

I am going on an extended trip for **one month**.

1157- ものの/monono [p] *although, despite*

大丈夫と言ったものの、本当は心配だ。

Although I said that it would be okay, I am worried.

1158- 展開/tenkai [n] *development*

思いがけない展開に驚く。

I am surprised by this unexpected **development**.

1159- 事業/jigyoo [n] *business, enterprise*

新しい事業を始める。

I am starting a new **business**.

1160- データ/deeta [n] *data*

データを改ざんしてはいけない。

You should not alter the **data**.

1161- 役/yaku [n] *part, role*

みんながお姫様の役をやりたがる。

Everyone wants to have the princess's **role**.

1162- 伸びる/nobiru [v] *grow, stretch, extend*

急に息子の背が伸びる。

My son started **growing** all the sudden.

1163- 通常/tsuujoo [adv] *normally, ordinary*

通常、六時に閉まる。

Normally, it closes at six o'clock.

1164- ピアノ/piano [n] *piano*

娘がピアノのレッスンを受けている。

My daughter is taking **piano** lessons.

1165- 行為/kooi [n] *action, behavior*

自分の**行為**に自分で責任を持つ。

Take responsibility for your own **actions**.

1166- 悩む/nayamu [v] *be worried*

経済的なことについて**悩む**。

I **am worried** about my finances.

1167- 第二/daini [n] *second, secondary*

ここは**第二**の故郷といえる。

This is my **second** hometown.

1168- 議論/giron [n] *argument, discussion, debate*

同僚と**議論**をする。

I am **debating** this with my colleagues.

1169- 記録/kiroku [n] *record*

コミュニケーションを**記録**する。

Keep a **record** of communications.

1170- 当てる/ateru [v] *hit, expose*

まとに**当てる**。

Hit the target.

1171- 出来事/dekigoto [n] *incident, happening*

めずらしい**出来事**が起きる。

An unusual **incident** happens.

1172- 温かい/atatakai [i-adj] *warm, mild*

温かい部屋でくつろぐ。

Relax in a **warm** room.

1173- おかげ/okage [n] *thanks, virtue*

おかげ様^{さま}でとても助^{たす}かりました。

Thanks so much for your help.

1174- 安全/anzen [n] *safety, security*

交通安全^{こうつうあんぜん}のキャンペーンをする。

Start a campaign for road **safety**.

1175- 眺める/nagameru [v] *view, gaze at*

ホテルの窓^{まど}から海^{うみ}を眺^{なが}める。

I enjoy **gazing at** the ocean from my hotel window.

1176- いかに/ikani [adv] *how, in what way*

いかに自分^{じぶん}が恵^{めぐ}まれているかと思^{おも}う。

How is it that I am so fortunate?

1177- 設置/secchi [n] *installation*

道路^{どうろ}に信号^{しんごう}が設置^{せっち}された。

Traffic lights were **installed** on the road.

1178- 極めて/kiwamete [adv] *extremely*

この問題^{もんだい}は極^{きわ}めて難^{むずか}しい。

This problem is **extremely** complicated.

1179- 入院/nyuuin [n] *hospitalization*

友人^{ゆうじん}の病気^{びょうき}は入院^{にゅういん}する必要^{ひつよう}がある。

My friend's illness requires **hospitalization**.

1180- 積極的/sekkyokuteki [na-adj] *active, aggressive*

地域^{ちいき}で積極的^{せっきょくてき}な役割^{やくわり}を担^{にな}う。

I take an **active** role in the community.

1181- 事故/jiko [n] *accident, incident*

事故の多い場所に気をつける。

Be aware of areas that have a lot of **accidents**.

1182- たたく/tataku [v] *slap, hit, clap*

ゲームでもぐらの頭をたたく。

In this game you **hit** moles on the head.

1183- としても/to-shitemo [cp] *even if*

大変だとしても、あきらめてはいけない。

Even if it is difficult, do not give up.

1184- 会話/kaiwa [n] *conversation*

彼女と楽しい会話をした。

I had a fun **conversation** with her.

1185- 方々/katagata [n] *people*

多くの方々が式に来た。

Many **people** came to the ceremony.

1186- 要る/iru [v] *need, want*

図書館で新しい本が要る。

The library **needs** new books.

1187- 鳥/tori [n] *bird, poultry, chicken*

庭で鳥に餌をやる。

I feed **chickens** in the yard.

1188- 何とか/nantoka [adv] *somehow, one way or another*

その仕事は何とか終わりました。

Somehow, we have managed to finish the task.

1189- 市/shi [n] *city*

小さな**市**が統合される。

Small **cities** are amalgamating.

1190- 眠る/nemuru [v] *sleep, die*

彼はいつも会議中に**眠る**。

He always **sleeps** during meetings.

1191- 自信/jishin [n] *self-confidence*

演説には**自信**がない。

I have no **confidence** in public speaking.

1192- 固い/katai [i-adj] *hard, solid, stiff*

硬いゆでたまごが好きだ。

I prefer **hard**-boiled eggs.

1193- 戦後/sengo [n] *postwar period*

日本の**戦後**の復興はすばらしい。

Japan's **postwar** recovery is amazing.

1194- 値段/nedan [n] *price, cost*

値段は相場で変わる。

The **price** changes with the market.

1195- 通じる/tsuujiru [v] *lead, communicate*

ハワイでは日本語が**通じる**。

Japanese can be used to **communicate** in Hawaii.

1196- 動かす/ugokasu [v] *move, shift*

ガレージの前の車を**動かす**。

Move the car that is in front of the garage.

1197- トイレ/toire [n] *toilet, restroom*

トイレに列ができている。

There is a line leading to the **restroom**.

1198- あんな/anna [adj] *such, like that*

あんなおもちゃがほしい。

I want a toy **like that**.

1199- 避ける/sakeru [v] *avoid*

渋滞を避ける。

I **avoid** traffic.

1200- お勧め/osusume [n] *recommendation, suggestion*

あなたへのお勧めはこちらです。

Here are my **recommendations** for you.

1201- 野球/yakyuu [n] *baseball*

中学校の野球チームでキャッチャーをしました。

I was a catcher for the **baseball** team in middle school.

1202- 穴/ana [n] *hole*

もぐらの穴がある。

There is a mole **hole**.

1203- クリック/kurikku [n] *click*

ボタンをクリックして次のページへ進む。

Click the button to go to the next page.

1204- 捕らえる/toraeru [v] *seize, capture*

どろぼうをおまわりさんが捕らえる。

The police **captures** the thief.

1205- 昨年/sakunen [n] *last year*

昨年は自然災害の多い年だった。

There were many natural disasters **last year**.

1206- 減少/genshoo [n] *decrease, reduction*

子供の数の減少は明らかです。

The **decrease** in the number of children is apparent.

1207- 洗う/arau [v] *wash*

流しで皿を洗う。

I **wash** my plates in the kitchen sink.

1208- 左/hidari [n] *left*

アメリカでは左ハンドルだ。

In America, the steering wheel is on the **left**.

1209- 珍しい/mezurashii [i-adj] *rare, unusual*

珍しい魚が見つかった。

An **unusual** fish was discovered.

1210- 尋ねる/tazuneru [v] *ask, enquire*

バス停までの道を尋ねる。

I will **ask for** directions to the bus stop.

1211- 一言/hitokoto [n] *a few words, brief comment*

うちの母はいつも一言多い。

My mom always has **a few words** to add.

1212- 男の子/otokonoko [n] *boy*

うるさい男の子がいる。

There is a noisy **boy** in here.

1213- 制度/seedo [n] *system, institution*

新しい介護保険の**制度**は複雑だ。

The new long-term care insurance **system** is too complicated.

1214- 買い物/kaimono [n] *shopping*

買い物は午前中に行くのがよい。

It's better to go **shopping** in the morning.

1215- チーム/chīmu [n] *team*

チームスポーツは協調性が養われる。

Team sports nurture cooperation.

1216- 登場/toojoo [n] *appearance*

お気に入りのキャラクターの**登場**が楽しみだ。

I look forward to my favorite character's **appearance**.

1217- 期間/kikan [n] *period, interval, time*

期間限定のセールをやっている。

There is a limited **time** sale.

1218- 金額/kingaku [n] *amount of money*

何回計算しても**金額**が合わない。

No matter how many times I count, the **amount of money** doesn't add up.

1219- 塩/shio [n] *salt*

塩とこしょうをかける。

Sprinkle **salt** and pepper.

1220- 奥/oku [n] *interior, inner part, deep*

山の**奥**に入る。

I go **deep** into the mountains.

1221- 九/kyuu [num] *nine*

九たす一は十だ。
Nine plus one is ten.

1222- まだまだ/madamada [adv] *still more*

まだまだやることがある。
There's **still more** to do.

1223- 習う/narau [v] *be taught, learn*

お習字を**習う**。
I'm **learning** calligraphy.

1224- 番組/bangumi [n] *show, program (T.V.)*

歴史番組をテレビで見る。
I watch history **programs on TV**.

1225- ひととき（一時）/hitotoki [adv] *at one time, for a while, a moment*

友人と楽しい**ひととき**を過ごす。
I had **some** fun **moments** with my friends.

1226- ケース /keesu [n] *case*

この**ケース**では弁護側は有利ではないんだ。
In this **case**, the defense is disadvantaged.

1227- 傾向/keekoo [n] *tendency, trend*

最近は結婚をしない**傾向**がある。
There is a **trend** lately of people not getting married.

1228- 日々/hibi [n] *daily, day after day*

日々の努力が報われる。
My **daily** efforts are being rewarded.

1229- 拡大(する)/kakudai (suru) [v] *enlarge, magnify, expand, amplify*

地図を拡大する。

Enlarge the map.

1230- レベル /reberu [n] *level, degree*

ゲームで次のレベルに進む。

I am progressing to the next **level** of the game.

1231- よろしく/yoroshiku [adv] *properly, best regards*

よろしくお願いします。

My **best regards** to you.

1232- 疑問/gimon [n] *question, doubt*

政治への疑問がある。

I have my **doubts** about politics.

1233- それなり/sorenari [n] *as it is, appropriate for, right for*

それなりの生活ができればよい。

I'd like to live the life that is **right for** me.

1234- 現状/genjoo [n] *current condition, current situation, status quo*

現状ではこれ以上は望めない。

We cannot expect anything more given the **current situation**.

1235- ドイツ/doitsu [n] *Germany*

ドイツのお城をたずねたい。

I want to visit the castles in **Germany**.

1236- 取り上げる/toriageru [v] *pick up, take up, feature*

記事でこの問題を取り上げる。

I will **take up** this issue in the article.

1237- 主に/omoni [adv] *mainly*

母が主に料理をします。

My mother **mainly** does the cooking.

1238- 伯母、叔母/oba [n] *aunt*

伯母は父の姉です。

My **aunt** is my father's big sister.

1239- パン/pan [n] *bread*

ランチにパンを買いにいく。

I will go buy some **bread** for lunch.

1240- クラス/kurasu [n] *class*

クラスに新しい生徒が来た。

A new student joined my **class**.

1241- 肉/niku [n] *flesh, meat*

オーブンで肉を焼く。

Cook **meat** in the oven.

1242- なるべく/narubeku [adv] *as much as possible*

なるべく早く家に帰りたい。

I want to get home **as** soon **as possible**.

1243- 指/yubi [n] *finger, toe*

指で数をかぞえる。

Count on your **fingers**.

167

1244- 態度/taido [n] *attitude, manner*

食事の態度を注意された。

I was warned for my poor table **manners**.

1245- 地/chi [n] *ground, land*

地に足をつけてがんばる。

Keep your feet on the **ground** and do your best.

1246- 全国/zenkoku [n] *nationwide*

この番組は全国放送です。

This program goes to air **nationwide**.

1247- 答え/kotae [n] *answer*

算数の問題の答えがわからない。

I don't know the **answer** to the math problem.

1248- 世話/sewa [n] *look after, help, take care*

赤ちゃんの世話で忙しい。

I am busy **taking care** of my baby.

1249- 差/sa [n] *difference, variation*

この値段の差は何ですか。

What is the **difference** in price?

1250- 一切/issai [n] *all, everything*

彼は仕事で一切手を抜かない。

He does not take any shortcuts at **all**.

1251- 食う/kuu [v] *eat, survive*

自然界のしくみは食うか食われるかだよ。

In nature it is either **eat** or be eaten.

1252- 文章/bunshoo [n] sentences, a piece of writing, text

文章はわかりやすく書きなさい。

Write your **sentences** in an easy-to-understand manner.

1253- 背景/haikee [n] background

背景の色がすごく綺麗だね。

The **background** colors are so beautiful.

1254- 負担/futan [n] *burden*

労働者階級の税負担が大きい。

A working class has a big tax **burden**.

1255- 事情/jijoo [n] *circumstances*

人にはそれぞれ事情がある。

Everyone has their own **circumstances**.

1256- メンバー/menbaa [n] member

野球のメンバーに選ばれた。

I have been chosen as a **member** of the baseball team.

1257- ようやく/yooyaku [adv] finally, at last

ようやくあなたの話がわかりました。

I **finally** understand what you mean.

1258- 地方/chihoo [n] countryside, region

地方と都会、どっちが住みやすいかな。

I wonder which is better to live in, the **countryside** or the city.

1259- 豊か/yutaka [na-adj] abundant, wealthy

あの国には豊かな天然資源があります。

The country has **abundant** natural resources.

1260- 助ける/tasukeru [v] save, help

困っている人を見たら、**助ける**のは当たり前だよ。

You should **help** when you see someone in trouble.

1261- 詰まる/tsumaru [v] *packed with, clogged*

水道管が**詰まる**。

The water pipe will get **clogged**.

1262- 一個/ikko [n] *a piece*

そのおもち、**一個**ちょうだい。

Can you give me a **piece** of mochi?

1263- 大阪/oosaka [n] *Osaka*

明日は**大阪**まで出張だ。

I am going to **Osaka** on a business trip tomorrow.

1264- 果たす/hatasu [v] *accomplish, fulfill*

親としての責任は**果たす**必要があります。

You need to **fulfill** your responsibilities as a parent.

1265- 支える/sasaeru [v] *support, sustain*

農業が国の輸出を**支える**。

Agriculture **supports** the country's exports.

1266- 抱える/kakaeru [v] hold or carry in the arms, have (problems)

厳しい締め切りのノルマを**抱える**。

I **have** a quota with a tight deadline.

1267- 大分/daibu [adv] considerably, greatly

会社の評判は**大分**良くなりました。

The company's reputation has improved **considerably**.

1268- 追う/ou [v] *chase, follow*

おいかけっこで友達を**追う**。

I'm **chasing** my friend in a game of tag.

1269- 権利/kenri [n] *right, privilege*

移民の**権利**を尊重する。

Respect the **rights** of immigrants.

1270- 何々/naninani [pron] *such and such, so and so (vague example)*

何々さんという名前の人から電話がありました。

There was a call from Mr. **so and so**.

1271- 計算/keesan [n] *calculation*

計算ミスをする。

Make a **calculation** error.

1272- 痛み/itami [n] *pain, ache*

寒い日は膝の**痛み**を感じる。

I feel **pain** in my knees on cold days.

1273- 返す/kaesu [v] *return, turn over*

間違えて届いた荷物を**返す**。

Return a package that was delivered in error.

1274- 庭/niwa [n] *garden, backyard, courtyard*

庭に花を植えましょう。

Let's plant some flowers in the **backyard**.

1275- 納得(する)/nattoku-suru [v] *consent, comprehend, understand, convince*

その判決は**納得**がいきません。

I cannot **comprehend** the judgement.

1276- 組織/soshiki [n] *organization, structure*

会社の**組織**図を見る。

Review the **organization** chart of the company.

1277- 能力/nooryoku [n] *ability , skill*

彼はいろいろな**能力**がある。

He has a wide range of **abilities**.

1278- 人口/jinkoo [n] *population*

その都市は**人口**が多い。

The city has a large **population**.

1279- 薄い/usui [i-adj] *thin, pale*

その**薄い**本は歴史の教科書ではありません。

The **thin** book is not a history textbook.

1280- 注/chuu [n] *annotation, remark, note*

注：時間は変更になることがあります。

Note: The time is subject to change.

1281- 二回/nikai [n] *twice*

英語のレッスンは週に**二回**です。

English lessons are **twice** a week.

1282- 治療/chiryoo [n] *(medical) treatment*

病院で怪我の**治療**を受けています。

I am getting **treatment** for my injury at the hospital.

1283- 昼/hiru [n] *noon, daytime, lunch*

明日の**昼**ごろ電話します。

I will call you tomorrow around **noon**.

1284- 通じて/tsuujite [adv] *through, via*

英語のレッスンを**通じて**異文化を学びます。

I learn about other cultures **through** my English lessons.

1285- せっかく/sekkaku [adv] *with effort, at great pains*

雨の中を**せっかく**歩いて行ったのに店が閉まっていた。

The store was closed, even though I **made the effort** to walk there in the rain.

1286- 赤い/akai [i-adj] *red*

赤組の子供は**赤い**帽子をかぶっています。

Children in the red group are wearing **red** caps.

1287- 比較的/hikakuteki [adv] *comparatively, relatively*

この老人ホームは**比較的**安い。

This nursing home is **relatively** cheap.

1288- サービス/saabisu [n] *service*

日本ではチップの代わりに**サービス**料を払う。

In Japan, you pay a **service** fee instead of a tip.

1289- 何人/nannin [n] *how many people?*

パーティには**何人**来ますか。

How many people are coming to the party?

1290- 荷物/nimotsu [n] *luggage, package*

荷物はどこで受け取れますか。

Where can I pick up my **luggage**?

1291- 魅力/miryoku [n] *charm, appeal, attractive*

これは我が社にとって**魅力**のある取引だ。

This is an **attractive** deal for our company.

1292- 現場/genba [n] *actual site*

工事現場の監督をする。

Supervise the construction **site**.

1293- 道具/doogu [n] *tool*

箱を作るにはどの道具を使えばいいですか。

Which **tools** should I use for making a box?

1294- 遠く/tooku [adv] *far, distant*

その街は私の住んでいるところから遠く離れています。

That town is **far** away from where I live.

1295- 中学/chuugaku [n] *middle school, junior high school*

中学の教科書は重い。

Middle school textbooks are heavy.

1296- 村/mura [n] *village*

フランスには美しい村がある。

France has beautiful **villages**.

1297- システム/shisutemu [n] *system, institution*

私のコンピューターはシステムのアップデートが必要だ。

My computer needs a **system** update.

1298- あそこ/asoko [pron] *there*

あそこを見て！

Look over **there**!

1299- 十時/juuji [n] *ten o'clock*

デパートが十時に開く。

The department store opens at **ten o'clock**.

1300- 息/iki [n] *breath*

寒いので息が白く見えます。

I can see my **breath** when it's cold.

1301- 伝わる/tsutawaru [v] *spread, descend, relay, communicate*

間違った情報が伝わる。

Incorrect information will be **relayed**.

1302- 撮影/satsuei [n] *shooting, filming, photographing*

映画の撮影が行われた。

A movie was being **filmed**.

1303- 指導/shidoo [n] *guidance, coaching, leadership*

カウンセラーの指導を受ける。

I am getting **guidance** from a counselor.

1304- 生かす/ikasu [v] *keep alive, make use of*

仕事に自分のスキルを生かす。

Make good **use of** your skills at work.

1305- 韓国/kankoku [n] *South Korea*

韓国の焼肉はおいしい。

Korean *yakiniku** is delicious.

*Grilled meat cuisine.

1306- 字/ji [n] *character, handwriting*

字はきれいに書きなさい。

Write your **characters** neatly.

1307- 指定(する)/shitei-suru [v] *designate, appoint*

指定の席につく。

Take your **designated** seat.

1308- 経営/kee'ee [n] *management, operation*

彼は会社の経営陣です。

He is a **management** team member of the company.

1309- あらゆる/arayuru [and] *every*

あらゆる可能な解決方法を検討してください。

Consider **every** possible solution.

1310- 価値/kachi [n] *value, worth*

値段と価値は同じではない。

Price and **value** are not the same.

1311- 南/minami [n] *south*

南の窓は眺めがよい。

We have a good view from the **south** window.

1312- 成立/seeritsu [n] arrangement, establishment, conclusion

商談が成立する。

The negotiations reached a **conclusion**.

1313- 季節/kisetsu [n] *season*

日本語では、四つの季節を四季という。

The four **seasons** are called *shiki* in Japanese.

1314- 導入/dounyuu [n] *introduction, installation*

あたらしい消費税率の導入が検討されている。

The **introduction** of a new consumption tax rate is being considered.

1315- ことにする/koto-ni-suru [aux] *decide to*

明日から朝は六時に起きることにする。

Starting tomorrow, I have **decided to** wake up at six in the morning.

1316- 一枚/ichi-mai [n] *one sheet, one slide*

紙を一枚もらえますか。
Can you give me **a sheet** of paper?

1317- い/i [p disc] *question (strengthens a question)*

なぜそんな事をしたんだい。
Why did you do such a thing?

1318- 先輩/senpai [n] *senior, elder*

中学の先輩に偶然会った。
I met one of the **seniors** from my junior high school by chance.

1319- 全員/zee'in [n] *everybody, all*

火事の際は全員が避難しなければなりません。
Everybody must evacuate in the event of fire.

1320- にしても/ni-shitemo [cp] *even if, even so*

それにしても、彼は遅いなあ。
Even so, he is still running late.

1321- 四人/yonin [n] *four people*

うちは子供二人の四人家族です。
We are a family of **four,** with two children.

1322- 人物/jinbutsu [n] *person, figure*

歴史上の人物に会いたい。

I wish I could meet an historical **figure**.

1323- 距離/kyori [n] *distance, range*

東京から大阪までの距離は約四百km です。

The **distance** from Tokyo to Osaka is about 400 km.

1324- 泊まる/tomaru [v] *stay at*

温泉旅館に泊まる。

We are **staying at** an inn with a hot spring.

1325- 充実(する)/juujitsu-suru [v] *enhance, enrich, fulfill*

充実した休日を過ごした。

I had a **fulfilling** holiday.

1326- によると/ni-yoruto [cp] *according to*

統計によると、少子化が進んでいる。

According to the statistics, the decline in the birthrate is accelerating.

1327- コミュニケーション/komyuunikeeshon [n] *communication*

ビジネスでコミュニケーションは大事だ。

Communication is important in business.

1328- 散歩/sanpo [n] *walk, stroll*

毎日犬の散歩に行く。

I **walk** my dog every day.

1329- グループ/guruupu [n] *group*

四人ずつのグループでカートに乗った。

We got on the carts in **groups** of four.

1330- 黒い/kuroi [i-adj] black

彼女は黒い服が似合う。
She looks good in **black**.

1331- 九時/kuji [n] *nine o'clock*

仕事は朝の九時からです。
My work starts at **nine o'clock** in the morning.

1332- 石/ishi [n] *stone, gem, jewel*

日本式の庭に大きな石を置く。
We place large **stones** in Japanese gardens.

1333- エネルギー/enerugii [n] *energy, stamina*

自然エネルギーの開発が進んでいる。
Development of natural **energy** is progressing.

1334- 挨拶/aisatsu [n] *greeting, salute*

新しいお客様に挨拶のメッセージを送る。
Send a **greeting** message to new customers.

1335- 愛/ai [n] *love, affection*

彼は愛国心を持っています。
He has a **love** for his country.

1336- 比較/hikaku [n] *comparison*

第一四半期の比較表をご覧ください。
Please see the chart for a **comparison** with the first quarter.

1337- 結ぶ/musubu [v] *tie, bind*

靴のひもを結ぶ。
Tie your shoelaces.

1338- 移る/utsuru [v] *move, change, transfer*

新しい部門に移る。

I am being **transferred** to a new division.

1339- 従来/juurai [n] *traditional, existing*

従来とは違う新しいアイディアが欲しい。

We want new ideas, something different from our **traditional** ones.

1340- 嫌い/kirai [na-adj] *dislike*

子供は暗い色が嫌いです。

Children **dislike** dark colors.

1341- 注目/chuumoku [n] *attention*

新しい地下アイドルが注目を集める。

New underground idols are getting some **attention**.

1342- 携帯/keetai [n] *portable, cell phone*

携帯の番号にショートメッセージを送ります。

I am sending a short message to your **cell phone** number.

1343- 休む/yasumu [v] *be absent, rest, take a day off.*

日陰で休む。

I am **resting** in the shade.

1344- 甘い/amai [i-adj] *sweet*

甘い言葉に騙されないように。

Don't be fooled by **sweet** words.

1345- 最高/saikoo [na-adj] *highest, supreme, the most*

最高のおもてなしでお客様を迎える。

We greet customers with the **highest** level of hospitality.

1346- 弟/otooto [n] *younger brother*

私には三歳下の弟がいる。

I have a **brother** three years **younger** than me.

1347- 卵/tamago [n] *egg*

にわとりが先か、卵が先か。

Which was first, the chicken or the **egg**?

1348- 服/fuku [n] *clothes*

去年買った子供服がもう小さい。

The children's **clothes** I bought last year are already too small.

1349- 赤ちゃん/akachan [n] *baby, infant*

赤ちゃんにお祝いを贈ろう。

Let's send a **baby** shower gift.

1350- 始め/hajime [n] *beginning, start*

「始め」の合図が聞こえたら行進をするように。

Start marching when you hear "**begin!**"

1351- 要求/yookyuu [n] *demand, firm request*

上司が無理な要求をする。

My boss makes unreasonable **demands**.

1352- 紙/kami [n] *paper*

紙の節約のために、デジタル配信をする。

Use digital distribution to save **paper**.

1353- 妹/imooto [n] *younger sister*

妹は私のドレスを着たがる。

My **younger sister** likes wearing my dresses.

1354- 額/gaku [n] *picture frame, amount of money*

この絵はゴールドの額が合う。
This painting looks good with a gold **frame**.

1355- 混ぜる/mazeru [v] *mix, stir, blend*

小麦粉と卵を混ぜる。
Mix flour and eggs.

1356- 抱く/idaku [v] *embrace, hold*

女の子が人形を抱く。
The girl is **holding** a doll.

1357- 出来上がる/dekiagaru [v] *be completed, be finished*

論文の下書きが出来上がる。
The draft of the essay **is complete**.

1358- 小説/shoosetsu [n] *novel*

受賞した小説を読んだ。
I read an award-winning **novel**.

1359- 訪れる/otozureru [v] *visit*

先祖の墓地を訪れる。
I **visit** my ancestor's grave.

1360- 汗/ase [n] *sweat*

シャツに汗のしみがある。
The shirt is stained with **sweat**.

1361- 特別/tokubetsu [na-adj] *special*

この服は特別セールで買った。
I bought these clothes at a **special** sale.

1362- 改善/kaizen [n] improvement

このプランは**改善**の余地がある。
There is room for **improvement** in this plan.

1363- 休み/yasumi [n] rest, vacation, holiday, day off

次の**休み**に山に行きます。
I will go to the mountains on my next **day off**.

1364- 咲く/saku [v] bloom

四月に桜の花が**咲く**。
The cherry blossoms **bloom** in April.

1365- 基本/kihon [n] foundation, basics, standard

スポーツはまず**基本**を練習した方がいいでしょう。
You should practice the **basics** first in any sport.

1366- 暑い/atsui [i-adj] hot, warm

京都の夏は**暑い**。
It's **hot** in Kyoto in summer.

1367- 向く/muku [v] face, turn toward

右に**向く**。
Turn toward the right.

1368- ますます/masumasu [adv] increasingly, more and more

結婚しない人が**ますます**増えています。
More and more people are choosing not to get married.

1369- 最終的 /saishuuteki [na-adj] final, eventual

最終的な判断は医者に任そう。

Let's trust the doctor with the **final** decision.

1370- 感情/kanjoo [n] *emotion, feeling*

子供の感情は大人と違う。

Children's **feelings** are different from those of adults.

1371- 我慢/gaman [n] *patience, endurance*

「石の上にも三年*」とは我慢の大切さのことだ。

The saying "three years on a stone" is about the importance of having **patience**.

*"Ishi no ue ni mo sannen" literally translates as "3 years on a stone," this is a proverb that implies that 3 years on a cold stone will make the stone warm, imploring the virtues of patience.

1372- 浮かぶ /ukabu [v] *float*

あひるのおもちゃが風呂に浮かぶ。

A rubber duck is **floating** in the tub.

1373- 利益/rieki [n] *profit, gains*

今期は利益が上がった。

Our **profit** increased this quarter.

1374- 先日/senjitsu [n] *the other day*

先日はありがとうございました。

Thank you for your help the other day.

1375- 裏/ura [n] *behind, rear, back*

家の裏に花壇があります。

There is a flower bed in the **back** of the house.

1376- もたらす/motarasu [v] *bring, cause*

台風が大きな被害をもたらす。

The typhoon **caused** great damage.

1377- 姉/ane [n] *older sister*

三歳年上の姉がいます。

I have a **sister** three years **older** than me.

1378- 問う/tou [v] *ask, inquire, accuse*

いじめの責任を学校に問う。

Accuse the school of having responsibility for the bullying.

1379- 継ぐ/tsugu [v] *succeed, take over*

父から家業を継ぐ。

I will **take over** the family business from my father.

1380- 北海道/Hokkaidoo [n] *Hokkaido*

北海道は本州の北にある。

Hokkaido is located north of *Honshu**.

*The main island of Japan where Tokyo, Osaka and Kyoto are located.

1381- 構成/koosee [n] *composition, structure*

プレゼンの構成を考えてください。

Please think through the **structure** of our presentation.

1382- 反応/hannoo [n] *reaction, response*

キャンペーンのお客さんの反応を見る。

We will see the customer **response** to the campaign.

1383- ナイフ/naifu [n] *knife*

ナイフでケーキを切る。

I cut the cake with a **knife**.

1384- 新宿/Shinjuku [n] *Shinjuku*

新宿に都庁がある。

The Tokyo Metropolitan Government Buildings are located in **Shinjuku**.

1385- 活用/katsuyoo [n] *application, use*

資源の違う活用について考える。

Think about an alternative **use** for our resources.

1386- 正直/shoojiki [n] *honesty*

子供に正直の大切さを教える。

Teach children the importance of **honesty**.

1387- 黒/kuro [n] *black*

黒のペイントで黒板を塗る。

Paint the blackboard with **black** paint.

1388- スーパー/suupaa [n] *supermarket*

帰りにスーパーで豆腐を買った。

I bought some tofu at the **supermarket** on my way home.

1389- プロ/puro [n] *professional*

プロの写真家にお見合い写真を撮ってもらった。

I had a **professional** photographer take a picture for a match maker.

1390- 渡す/watasu [v] *hand over, give, pass over*

切符を駅員に渡す。

You **hand** your ticket **over** to the station staff.

186

1391- 掲げる/kakageru [v] *publish, hang out, hold up, display*

運動のスローガンを掲げる。

Display the movement's slogan.

1392- 京都/kyooto [n] *Kyoto*

京都には美しい寺がいっぱいある。

There are many beautiful temples in **Kyoto**.

1393- 就職/shuushoku [n] *job hunting, employment*

今年は就職がとても厳しい。

Students are having great difficulty finding **employment** this year.

1394- 立派/rippa [na-adj] *great, splendid*

甥が立派な青年に育った。

My nephew grew up to be a **splendid** young man.

1395- 舞台/butai [n] *stage, scene*

ミュージカルの舞台を観た。

We saw a musical **scene**.

1396- 現地/genchi [n] *on site, local*

現地にスタッフがいます。

There are local staff **on site**.

1397- 数字/suuji [n] *number, figure*

シートに数字を入力する。

Enter **figures** into the sheet.

1398- 提出/teeshutsu [n] *submission*

課題の提出の締め切りは今日です。

The **submission** deadline for the assignment is today.

1399- コンピューター/konpyuutaa [n] *computer*

ラップトップの**コンピューター**を買いました。

I bought a laptop **computer**.

1400- 東京都/Tookyoo-to [n] *Tokyo*

東京都は日本の首都です。

Tokyo is the capital of Japan.

1401- 弾く/hiku [v] *play (musical instrument)*

コンクールでバイオリンを**弾く**。

I will **play** the violin at the competition.

1402- 自宅/jitaku [n] *one's home, house*

今夜は**自宅**に帰りません。

I am not returning **home** tonight.

1403- 腹/hara [n] *belly, stomach*

お父さんはビール**腹**です。

My father has a beer **belly**.

1404- 喜び/yorokobi [n] *pleasure, delight*

喜びでいっぱいです。

I am filled with pleasure.

1405- しょうがない/shoo-ga-nai [cp] *can't be helped, inevitable, unavoidable*

彼の遅刻する癖は**しょうがない**。

He **can't help** his habit of being late.

1406- しようがない/shiyoo-ga-nai [cp] *can't be helped, inevitable, unavoidable*

それは**しようがない**問題だ。
It is an **unavoidable** problem.

1407- 風呂/furo [n] *bath*

朝のお**風呂**が好きです。
I like taking a **bath** in the morning.

1408- 香り/kaori [n] *smell, scent*

森の**香り**の風呂が好きです。
I like the forest-**scented** bath.

1409- スキー/sukii [n] *ski*

スキーのゴーグルを買った。
I bought a pair of **ski** googles.

1410- 構う/kamau [v] *mind, care about*

小さな子供達を**構う**。
Care about the small children.

1411- 受け入れる/ukeireru [v] *accept, receive*

謝罪を**受け入れる**。
We **accept** your apology.

1412- お菓子/okashi [n] *sweets, snack food*

お菓子作りのクラスに行っています。
I am going to a **sweet**-making class.

1413- 無料/muryoo [n] *no charge, free*

無料の体験レッスンを受けました。
I took a **free** trial lesson.

1414- 付き合い/tsukiai [n] *socializing, association*

あのエージェントとは付き合いがある。

I have an **association** with the agent.

1415- 私共/watashidomo [pron] *we*

私共はその意見には反対です。

We are opposed to that opinion.

1416- 被害/higai [n] *damage, harm*

私の家は地震で大きな被害を受けました。

My home suffered major **damage** from the earthquake.

1417- 椅子/isu [n] *chair*

肘かけのある椅子が好きです。

I like sitting in the **chair** with the armrests.

1418- 直す/naosu [v] *fix, repair*

時計を直す。

I am **repairing** my watch.

1419- 桜/sakura [n] *cherry tree, cherry blossom*

桜は日本のシンボルの花です。

The **cherry blossom** is a symbolic flower in Japan.

1420- 解答/kaitoo [n] *answer, respond*

この問題の解答は裏のページに書いてあります。

The **answers** are printed on the back page.

1421- ゲーム /geemu [n] *game*

彼はコンピューターゲームに熱中している。

He is passionate about his computer **games**.

1422- ことはない/kotowanai [aux] *there is no need for*

<ruby>何<rt>なん</rt></ruby>も<ruby>心配<rt>しんぱい</rt></ruby>することはない。
There is no need to worry.

1423- 個人的 /kojinteki [na-adj] *personal, private*

<ruby>個人的<rt>こじんてき</rt></ruby>な<ruby>意見<rt>いけん</rt></ruby>は<ruby>控<rt>ひか</rt></ruby>えた<ruby>方<rt>ほう</rt></ruby>がいい。
You should refrain from voicing your **personal** opinions.

1424- 活躍/katsuyaku (suru) [n] *active, action*

<ruby>祖父<rt>そふ</rt></ruby>は<ruby>未<rt>いま</rt></ruby>だに<ruby>活躍<rt>かつやく</rt></ruby>している。
My grandfather is still **active**.

1425- 試験/shiken [n] *exam, test*

<ruby>運転免許<rt>うんてんめんきょ</rt></ruby>の<ruby>試験<rt>しけん</rt></ruby>を<ruby>受<rt>う</rt></ruby>ける。
I am going to take my driver's license **test**.

1426- 身近/mijika [na-adj] *close, familiar*

<ruby>身近<rt>みぢか</rt></ruby>な<ruby>人<rt>ひと</rt></ruby>に<ruby>相談<rt>そうだん</rt></ruby>する。
Get help from someone **close** to you.

1427- 苦しい/kurushii [i-adj] *hard, difficult*

<ruby>今<rt>いま</rt></ruby>は<ruby>経済的<rt>けいざいてき</rt></ruby>に<ruby>苦<rt>くる</rt></ruby>しい。
I am having a **hard** time economically.

1428 - 恥ずかしい/hazukashii [i-adj] *ashamed, embarrassed*

ドレスコードを<ruby>間違<rt>まちが</rt></ruby>えて<ruby>恥<rt>はず</rt></ruby>ずかしい。
I am **embarrassed** that I have mistaken the dress code.

1429- 検査/kensa [n] *inspection*

<ruby>市<rt>し</rt></ruby>が<ruby>下水道<rt>げすいどう</rt></ruby>の<ruby>検査<rt>けんさ</rt></ruby>をする。
My city is **inspecting** the sewers.

1430- 皮/kawa [n] *skin*

日焼けした皮がむける。

Sunburned **skin** will peel off.

1431- 白/shiro [n] *white, innocent*

容疑者は白だった。

The suspect was **innocent**.

1432- 足りる /tariru [v] *be sufficient, be enough*

用意した食べ物で足りる。

The food we brought **is enough** for everyone.

1433- 代表/daihyoo [n] *representative*

チームの代表がコメントを言う。

A **representative** of the team will make a comment.

1434- 夕方/yuugata [n] *evening, dusk*

夕方に夕焼けを見るのが好きだ。

I like watching sunsets in the **evening**.

1435- 下がる/sagaru [v] *fall, drop*

夜は気温が下がる。

The temperature **drops** at night.

1436- 実感/jikkan (suru) [v] *actually feel, deeply feel*

冬の寒さを実感する。

I am **really feeling** the winter cold.

1437- 有する/yuusuru [v] *have, own*

彼は大きな資産を有する。

He **owns** substantial assets.

1438- 抜く/nuku [v] *pull out, extract*

とげを**抜く**。

Pull out the thorns.

1439- 回す/mawasu [v] *turn, rotate*

時計の針を**回す**。

Turn the clock hand.

1440- 敵/teki [n] *enemy, opponent*

敵と戦う。

Fight against your **enemies**.

1441- 側/gawa [n] *side*

こちら**側**に並んでください。

Please line up on this **side**.

1442- 分かれる/wakareru [v] *divide, split*

道が**分かれる**。

The road **splits** up ahead.

1443- 見つめる/mitsumeru [v] *stare, gaze*

夜空の星を**見つめる**。

I **gaze at** the stars in the night sky.

1444- 祭り/matsuri [n] *festival*

夏**祭り**では盆踊りを楽しみます。

People enjoy the "bon odori" dancing at the summer **festival**.

1445- 抜ける/nukeru [v] *come loose, fall out*

髪が**抜ける**。

My hair is **falls out**.

193

1446- 仕様/shiyoo [n] *specification, style*

アプリの仕様について読んでください。

Read the app's **specifications**.

1447- 最大/saidai [n] *biggest, largest*

最大の恐竜の骨が発見された。

The **largest** ever dinosaur fossil was found.

1448- スタート/sutaato [n] *start*

スタートラインに立つ。

Stand at the **starting** line.

1449- なり/nari [p] *whether or not, or*

お風呂に入るなり夕食を食べるなりしてください。

Please either eat your dinner **or** take a bath.

1450- 沖縄/okinawa [n] *Okinawa*

沖縄は美しい海に囲まれています。

Okinawa is surrounded by beautiful ocean.

1451- 設ける/mookeru [v] *set up, prepare, create*

遊園地にベビーカー置き場を設ける。

Stroller parking areas have been **set up** at the amusement park.

1452- 幼稚園/yoochien [n] *preschool, kindergarten*

うちの四歳の子があの幼稚園に通っています。

My four-year-old goes to that **kindergarten**.

1453- 二度/nido [n] *twice*

週に二度レッスンを受ける。
I take lessons **twice** a week.

1454- 処理（する）/shori-suru [v] *process, manage, handle*

お客様のクレームの処理をする。
Handle customer complaints.

1455- 困難/konnan [n] *difficulty*

困難を克服する。
Overcome **difficulties**.

1456- あくまで/akumade [adv] *to the end, after all, stubbornly*

彼はあくまで間違いを認めない。
He **stubbornly** does not admit his errors.

1457- 分野/bun'ya [n] *field, discipline*

先端科学の分野で働く。
I work in the **field** of advanced science.

1458- 間違う/machigau [v] *make a mistake, be mistaken*

田中さんと中田さんを間違う。
We were **mistaken** and mixed up Mr. Tanaka and Mr. Nakata.

1459- 姿勢/shisee [n] *posture*

姿勢を正す。
Correct your **posture**.

1460- ショック/shokku [na-adj] *shock*

ショックなニュースを聞く。

I heard some **shocking** news.

1461- 暇/hima [n] *spare time, free time*

暇な時に電話をください。

Please give me a call when you have some **spare time**.

1462- つい/tsui [adv] *unintentionally, without thinking*

つい言い訳を言ってしまった。

I made an excuse **without thinking**.

1463- 土/tsuchi [n] *soil, dirt, ground*

土に種をまきました。

I sowed the **soil**.

1464- 隠す/kakusu [v] *hide, conceal*

宝物を隠す。

Hide the treasure.

1465- 緊張/kinchoo [n] *tension*

二人の間に緊張が走った。

There was **tension** between the two of them.

1466- それとも/soretomo [conj] *or*

コーヒーがいいですか、それとも紅茶がいいですか。

Would you like coffee **or** tea?

1467- 帰り/kaeri [n] *return*

犬が飼い主の帰りを待つ。

The dog waits for its owner's **return**.

1468- 三日/mikka [n] *the third day of the month*

家賃の期日は毎月三日です。

The rent is due on **the third** of every month.

1469- 戦う/tatakau [v] *fight*

勝つまで戦う。

I will keep **fighting** until I win.

1470- 単に/tanni [adv] *simply, only, solely*

単に真実を伝えたかった。

I **simply** wanted to tell the truth.

1471- 席/seki [n] *seat*

席についてください。

Please take a **seat**.

1472- つる/tsuru [v] *hang*

絵をつる。

I will **hang** the painting up.

1473- 達する/tassuru [v] *reach*

参加者が千人に達する。

The number of attendees will **reach** one thousand.

1474- 小学生/shoogakusee [n] *elementary school student*

小学生が学校へ向かって並んで歩いています。

Elementary school students are walking in line towards the school.

1475- ついに/tsuini [adv] *finally, at last*

ついに大学の学位を取得しました。

Finally, I got my college degree.

1476- 具合/guai [n] *condition*

エンジンの**具合**が悪い。

The **engine** is in a bad condition.

1477- 歯/ha [n] *tooth, teeth*

食後に**歯**を磨きなさい。

Brush your **teeth** after your meal.

1478- ベッド/beddo [n] *bed*

ベッドの上でジャンプしないでください。

Do not jump on the **bed**.

1479- 無事/buji [n] *safety, peace*

山での遭難者の**無事**を祈る。

Pray for the **safety** of the people lost in the mountains.

1480- 身体/shintai [n] *body, person*

身体を鍛える。

Strengthen your **body**.

1481- 何年/nannen [n] *what year? how many years?*

日本に行ったのは**何年**ですか。

What year did you go to Japan?

1482- 星/hoshi [n] *star*

今夜は**星**がきれいに見える。

The **stars** look bright tonight.

1483- 携帯電話/keetaidenwa [n] *cell phone, mobile phone*

携帯電話をスマホに変えます。

I am switching my **mobile phone** to a smart phone.

1484- 砂糖/satoo [n] *sugar*

私はコーヒーに砂糖を入れません。
I don't take **sugar** in my coffee.

1485- 切れる/kireru [v] *expire, run out*

これは賞味期限が切れる。
The food is about to **expire**.

1486- 維持（する）/iji-suru [v] *maintain, preserve*

寺を維持するにはコストがかかります。
It costs money to **preserve** the temples.

1487- 高さ/takasa [n] *height*

椅子の高さを計る。
Measure the **height** of the chair.

1488- 太陽/taiyoo [n] *sun*

夏は太陽がまぶしい。
The **sun** is bright in summer.

1489- 会場/kaijoo [n] *hall, site*

会場に多くの人がいた。
There were a lot of people in the **hall**.

1490- 素敵/suteki [na-adj] *lovely, nice*

素敵な人に会えて嬉しい。
I am glad to have met such **nice** people.

1491- 湯/yu [n] *hot water, warm water*

お風呂のお湯を沸かす。
Heat up the bath to get **hot water**.

1492- そもそも/somosomo [adv] *in the first place*

そもそも君がそれを始めた。

You started it **in the first place**.

1493- 約束/yakusoku [n] *promise*

約束は守るべきだ。

You should keep your **promises**.

1494- ワイン/wain [n] *wine*

赤と白のどちらのワインがいいですか。

Which **wine** would you like, red or white?

1495- 高校生 /kookoosee [n] *high school student*

高校生に人気があるのは何ですか。

What is popular among **high school students**?

1496- イベント/ibento [n] *event*

今週末は音楽のイベントがある。

There is a music **event** this weekend.

1497- 二日/futsuka [n] *two days*

この仕事に二日で慣れました。

I got used to this job in **two days**.

1498- 売れる/ureru [v] *be sold, sell*

このキャラクター商品はよく売れる。

This character product **sells** well.

1499- 少なくとも/sukunakutomo [adv] *at least*

この建設には少なくとも二年はかかる。

It will take **at least** two years to complete this development.

1500- 米国/beekoku [n] *United States*

米国から牛肉を輸入する。

Import beef from **the United States.**

1501- 周囲/shuui [n] *surroundings, around (you)*

周囲の人の意見を聞く。

Listen to the opinion of the people **around** you.

1502- 伺う/ukagau [v] *ask, inquire (humble)*

詳しい話を伺う。

I **asked** for more information.

1503- 引っ越す/hikkosu [n] *move (residence)*

仕事のために引っ越す。

We are **moving** for work.

1504- 二十年 nijuu-nen [n] *twenty years*

バブル後の二十年は経済的に失われた。

Economic growth stagnated for **twenty years** after the bubble.

1505- たまる/tamaru [v] *collect, accumulate*

お店のポイントがたまる。

My store points are **accumulating.**

1506- 精神的/seishinteki [na-adj] *spiritual, mental*

家族が精神的な支えになっています。

My family provides **spiritual** support to me.

1507- 中学校/chuugakkoo [n] *middle school, junior high school*

中学校は高校の隣にある。

My **middle school** is next to the high school.

1508- 仲良く/nakayoku [adv] *friendly, get along*

クラスメートとは仲良くしなさい。

Be **friendly** to your classmates.

1509- 言い方/iikata [n] *way of saying*

言い方に気をつけなさい。

Be careful of the **way you say** things.

1510- バランス/baransu [n] *balance*

ヨガでバランスボールに座るのが好きです。

I like sitting on a **balance** ball at yoga.

1511- 五年/gonen [n] *five years*

この会社で働き始めてもう五年になる。

It's been **five years** since I began working for this company.

1512- 安定/antee [n] *stability*

新しいバージョンでは安定性が向上しています。

The new version has improved **stability**.

1513- 完成/kansee [n] *completion*

家の完成が待ちきれない。

I can't wait for **completion** of our new house.

1514- 我が家/wagaya [n] *one's house*

我が家は角にあります。
Our house is on the corner of the block.

1515- 見かける/mikakeru [v] *see*

時々、駅で友達を見かける。
Sometimes, I see my friends at the station.

1516- 広げる/hirogeru [v] *spread, expand*

ピクニックシートを広げる。
I will spread out a picnic blanket.

1517- 参考/sankoo [n] *reference*

参考になる資料をさがす。
I am looking for some reference material.

1518- たとえ/tatoe [adv] *even if*

たとえ勝てなくても、ゲームに参加する。
Even if you can't win, join the game.

1519- 受け取る/uketoru [v] *get, accept, receive*

隣の人への荷物を受け取る。
I receive packages for the next-door neighbor.

1520- 冷たい/tsumetai [i-adj] *cold*

冬は北風が冷たい。
The north wind is cold in winter.

1521- 望む/nozomu [v] *hope*

明るい未来を望む。
I hope for a bright future.

1522- 適用/tekiyoo (suru) [v] *apply*

来週から新しい税率を適用しないといけない。

Starting next week, we need to **apply** the new tax rates.

1523- 宗教/shuukyoo [n] *religion*

宗教は個人の自由だ。

Individuals have the freedom to practice their **religion**.

1524- 一年間/ichinenkan [n] *for one year*

一年間は見習いだ。

I observed and learned every day **for one year**.

1525- 範囲/han'i [n] *range*

予算の範囲を決める。

Set a budget **range**.

1526- 接する/sessuru [v] *come in contact, meet*

私は仕事で外国人と接する機会が多い。

I have a lot of opportunities to **meet** foreigners at work.

1527- 戻す/modosu [v] *put back, restore*

使った道具は元に戻すように。

Please **put back** the tools you used.

1528- すっかり/sukkari [adv] *completely*

部屋がすっかりきれいになった。

The room has been **completely** cleaned up.

1529- 低下(する)/teika (suru) [v] *decline, drop*

気温が低下する。

The temperature is **dropping**.

1530- 政治/seeji [n] *politics*

政治に関心のない人が多い。

Many people are not interested in **politics**.

1531- なんら/nanra [adv] *nothing, whatever*

なんら変わっていない。

Nothing has been changed.

1532- 取り組む/torikumu [v] *tackle, engage in*

政府が税改革に取り組む。

The government is **engaged in** tax reforms.

1533- 余裕/yoyuu [n] *surplus, flexibility, room*

予算に余裕がない。

There is no **flexibility** in the budget.

1534- パリ/pari [n] *Paris (France)*

一度パリに住んでみたい。

I would love to live in **Paris** at least once.

1535- にて/nite [p case] *by, in, at, with*

これにて、会議を終了します。

With that, the meeting is dismissed.

1536- 奥さん/okusan [n] *wife*

友人に奥さんを紹介された。

My friend introduced his **wife** to me.

1537- 遅れる/okureru [v] *be late, de delayed*

学校に遅れる。

I am **late** for school.

1538- 担当/tantoo (suru) [v] *be in charge of*

私 はお客様サービスの担当です。

I **am in charge of** customer service.

1539- 向上/koojoo [n] *improvement, progress*

質の向上に努めています。

We are working to make an **improvement** in quality.

1540- 機械/kikai [n] *machine*

この工場ではすべての作業は機械によって 行 われています。

All the work in this factory is done by **machines**.

1541- 寄る/yoru [v] *stop by*

帰りにスーパーに寄る。

I will **stop by** the grocery store on my way home.

1542- 都市/toshi [n] *city*

都市計画が承認された。

The **city** plan has been approved.

1543- 費用/hiyoo [n] *cost, expense*

その費用は税控除されます。

The **expense** is tax deductible.

1544- 運転/unten [n] *driving, operation*

安全運転を常に心がけよう。

Always keep your mind on **driving** safely.

1545- 生地/kiji [n] *fabric (cloth material), dough*

パン屋は朝早くパン生地を作ります。

Bakers make their bread **dough** early in the morning.

1546- さあ/saa [conj] *now*

さあ、始めよう。
Now, let's start!

1547- だけでなく/dakedenaku [cp] *not only*

彼女は容姿だけでなく性格も素晴らしい。
She **not only** looks beautiful, but also has a wonderful personality.

1548- 予想/yosoo [n] *expectation, prediction*

私たちの予想以上の結果でした。
The result surpassed our **expectation**s.

1549- 一層/issoo [adv] *more, further*

一層のサービスの向上に努めます。
We will work to **further** improve our services.

1550- 旦那/danna [n] *husband*

うちの旦那は子供好きです。
My **husband** likes children.

1551- 経る/heru [v] *pass, go through, experience, go by*

時を経るにつれて、記憶も変わる。
As time **goes by**, memories change.

1552- 揃う/sorou [v] *become complete, become a full set*

好きな本が全部揃う。
The collection of my favorite books **is** now **complete**.

1553- 下げる/sageru [v] *lower, drop*

血圧を下げる薬を飲んでいます。
I am taking pills to **lower** my blood pressure.

1554- 誘う/sasou [v] *invite*

友達を映画に誘う。

I will **invite** my friend to a movie.

1555- 重ねる/kasaneru [v] *stack, layer*

ホットケーキをお皿の上で重ねる。

Stack the pancakes on the plate.

1556- 採用/saiyoo [n] *recruitment, employment, adoption*

新規採用を担当しています。

I am in charge of new **recruitment**.

1557- 価格/kakaku [n] *price*

ショッピングサイトで価格を比べる。

Compare **price**s on shopping sites.

1558- 飾る/kazaru [v] *decorate*

クリスマスツリーにオーナメントを飾る。

We **decorate** the Christmas tree with ornaments.

1559- がん/gan [n] *cancer*

がんの新薬が開発された。

A new **cancer** drug has been developed.

1560- 週/shuu [n] *week*

来週会いましょう。

Let's meet next **week**.

1561- 細い/hosoi [i-adj] *narrow, slender*

この細い道を抜けると大通りだ。

When you come out of this **narrow** street, you will come upon the main road.

1562- なおる/naoru [v] *be healed, get well, be repaired*

腰痛がなおる。

My back pain **has been healed**.

1563- 単純/tanjun [na-adj] *simple*

単純なシステムでわかりやすい。

The system is **simple** and easy to understand.

1564- ファックス/fakkusu [n] *fax*

メールではなくファックスを送ります。

I will send you a **fax** instead of an email.

1565- アルバイト/arubaito [n] *part-time job*

コンビニでアルバイトをする。

I have a **part-time job** at a convenience store.

1566- 北/kita [n] *north*

地図の北を上にする。

Turn the map **north** side up.

1567- 一生/isshoo [n] *life*

仕事に一生を捧げる。

I dedicate my **life** to my work.

1568- ファン/fan [n] *fan*

動画を観たファンの数が増えている。

The number of **fan**s who have watched the video is increasing.

1569- 及ぶ/oyobu [v] *reach*

山火事が住宅地に**及ぶ**。

The wildfires have **reach**ed a residential area.

1570- 調子/chooshi [n] *condition, tone*

体の**調子**が良くなった。

My **condition** has improved.

1571- 基準/kijun [n] *standard*

その器機は安全**基準**を満たしていません。

The equipment does not meet the safety **standards**.

1572- 植物/shokubutsu [n] *plant*

週に一度、室内**植物**に水をやる。

I water my indoor **plants** once a week.

1573- 契約/keeyaku [n] *contract*

レンタル**契約**を結ぶ。

I signed on a rental **contract**.

1574- 組む/kumu [v] *pair with*

彼とチームを**組む**。

I **paired** up **with** him.

1575- 叫ぶ/sakebu [v] *shout, scream*

彼は怒ると**叫ぶ**。

He **shouts** when he gets angry.

1576- 若者/wakamono [n] *youth, young people*

ビーチは**若者**で賑わっている。

The beach is filled with **young people**.

1577- 手段/shudan [n] *means, method*

違う手段をためしてみる。

Let's try a different **method**.

1578- 下ろす/orosu [v] *take down, withdraw*

棚から箱を下ろす。

Take the box **down** from the shelf.

1579- 明治/meeji [n] *Meiji (period)*

明治時代は日本で産業が発達した。

During the **Meiji era**, many industries were developed in Japan.

1580- 形成/keesee [n] *formation*

その学校は人格形成を目的としている。

The school's goal is the **formation** of a strong character.

1581- マンガ/manga [n] *comics, cartoon*

週刊のマンガを駅の売店で買う。

I buy weekly **comics** at the station kiosk.

1582- ドラマ/dorama [n] *drama*

月曜の夜はテレビでドラマを見る。

I watch **dramas** shows on television on Monday nights.

1583- いよいよ/iyoiyo [adv] *finally, at last*

いよいよドラマのクライマックスだ。

Finally, the drama has reached its climax.

1584- 高齢者/kooreesha [n] *elderly, senior citizen*

高齢者に電車の席を譲る。

On the train, you offer your seat to **the elderly**.

1585- 無駄/muda [n] *waste*

食べ物を無駄にしない。
Don't **waste** food.

1586- 髪/kami [n] *hair*

髪をのばしています。
I am letting my **hair** grow long.

1587- 管理/kanri (suru) [v] *control, management*

在庫管理システムに新しい商品を入力します。
Enter the new products into the inventory **management** system.

1588- サッカー/sakkaa [n] *football, soccer*

日曜は息子のサッカーの試合を見に行きます。
I am going to see my son's **soccer** game this Sunday.

1589- 工場/koojoo [n] *factory*

車の工場で働く。
I work at a car **factory**.

1590- 正確/seekaku [na-adj] *correct, accurate*

正確な到着時刻が画面に表示されます。
An **accurate** arrival time is displayed on the screen.

1591- 夫婦/fuufu [n] *married couple, spouse*

夫婦で税金申告をする。
We file our tax return as a **married couple**.

1592- 監督/kantoku [n] *director, manager, supervisor*

私は工事現場の監督です。
I am a **supervisor** at a construction site.

212

1593- 鍋/nabe [n] *pot*

冬は鍋料理がおいしい。
Hot-**pot** dishes are delicious in winter.

1594- バイト/baito [n] *part-time job*

私はファーストフードのレストランで**バイト**をしています。
I have a **part-time job** at a fast-food restaurant.

1595- 外す/hazusu [v] *remove, take off, unfasten*

安全ベルトを**外す**。
Remove your safety belt.

1596- 何でも/nandemo [adv] *anything*

わからない事は**何でも**聞いてください。
Please ask me **anything** that you don't understand.

1597- 階段/kaidan [n] *stairs*

エレベーターの代わりに**階段**を利用してください。
Take the **stairs** instead of the elevator.

1598- オーストラリア/oosutoraria [n] *Australia*

オーストラリアにはコアラがいる。
There are koalas in **Australia**.

1599- そこで/sokode [conj] *so, accordingly, therefore*

そこで、計画が変更されました。
Accordingly, our plan was revised.

1600- オーケー/ookee [n] *O.K., Okay*

オーケー、いいよ。
Okay, that's all right.

1601- 発達/hattatsu [n] *development*

幼児の**発達**を専攻しています。

I major in early childhood **development**.

1602- 適当/tekitoo [na-adj] *proper, suitable*

適当な量の塩を入れる。

Add the **proper** amount of salt.

1603- 戦い/tatakai [n] *fight, battle*

戦いのゲームが好きだ。

I like **fighting** games.

1604- はさむ/hasamu [v] *put in between, insert*

パンにハムを**はさむ**。

Put ham **in between** the bread.

1605- 鼻/hana [n] *nose*

花に**鼻**を近づける。

Bring your **nose** closer to the flower.

1606- 会/kai [n] *meeting, gathering*

カラオケの**会**に行った。

I went to a karaoke **gathering**.

1607- 数年/suunen [n] *several years*

博士号を取得するのに**数年**かかりました。

It took me **several years** to get my doctorate.

1608- 現代/gendai [n] *present day, modern times*

現代史よりも古代史が好きだ。

I prefer ancient history to **modern** history.

1609- 回復/kaifuku [n] *recovery*

一日も早いご回復をお祈りしています。

I am wishing for your quick **recovery**.

1610- すみません/sumimasen [interj] *excuse me, I am sorry*

すみません、手伝っていただけますか。

Excuse me, can you help me?

1611- コーヒー/koohii [n] *coffee*

朝はコーヒーを飲みます。

I have a cup of **coffee** in the morning.

1612- 塗る/nuru [v] *spread, paint*

パンにバターを塗る。

Spread some butter on your bread.

1613- 老人/roojin [n] *old person*

老人が公園で散歩している。

An **old man** is walking in the park.

1614- 共通/kyootsuu [n] *common*

私たちには共通の点がある。

We have something in **common**.

1615- 一瞬/isshun [n] *a moment, an instant*

彼は一瞬で間違いを見抜いた。

He spotted a mistake in **an instant**.

1616- 面倒/mendoo [na-adj] *troublesome, annoying*

面倒な仕事を受けてしまった。

I have taken on an **annoying** job.

1617- 開始/kaishi [n] *beginning, start*

開始時間は何時ですか。

What is the **start** time?

1618- 翌日/yokujitsu [n] *next day*

乗り継ぎ後、翌日の便に乗ります。

I have a layover and will board the **next day**.

1619- 商店街/shootengai [n] *shopping district, shopping strip*

地域の商店街よりも量販店は人気がある。

Mass retailers are more popular than local **shopping districts**.

1620- 原則/gensoku [n] *principle, general rule*

原則として、子供の入場を禁止しています。

The **general rule** is to prohibit the admission of children.

1621- 販売/hanbai [n] *sale*

今年は不動産の販売が好調だ。

Real estate **sales** are strong this year.

1622- 諦める/akirameru [v] *give up, quit*

健康のために飲酒を諦める。

I **quit** drinking for my health.

1623- 場面/bamen [n] *scene*

好きな場面を何度も観た。

I watched my favorite **scenes** many times.

216

1624- 障害/shoogai [n] *obstacle, handicap*

彼は障害を乗り越えて成功した。

He overcame his **handicap** and became successful.

1625- やや/yaya [adv] *slightly, a little*

我々のチームがやや負けている。

The team is losing by **a little**.

1626- 一定/ittee [n] *certain, constant*

彼は一定のペースで仕事をする。

He works at a **constant** pace.

1627- いかが/ikaga [adv] *how*

こちらのケーキはいかがですか。

How about this cake?

1628- 上手/joozu [n] *skillful, good, proficient*

彼女はピアノが上手だ。

She is **good** at playing piano.

1629- 関連/kanren [n] *relation, connection*

議題に関連して、議長はコメントした。

The Chair made a comment in **relation** to the agenda of the meeting.

1630- 笑顔/egao [n] *smile*

笑顔の素敵な人に会った。

I met someone with a pretty **smile**.

1631- 真ん中/mannaka [n] *middle*

道の真ん中でころんだ。

I fell over in the **middle** of the street.

1632- ビール/biiru [n] *beer*

冷たい**ビール**が好きだ。
I like cold **beer**.

1633- 正月/shoogatsu [n] *New Year*

正月にはお年玉をもらうのが楽しみだ。
I am looking forward to receiving *Otoshidama* on **New Year**'s Day.

1634- すら/sura [p] *even*

息子は算数が苦手で、足し算**すら**出来ない。
My son is not good at arithmetic, he can't **even** do addition.

1635- デザイン/dezain [n] *design*

新しいスマホの**デザイン**が話題になる。
A new smartphone **design** has become a hot topic.

1636- わざわざ/wazawaza [adv] *take the trouble*

わざわざお越しいただいてありがとうございます。
Thank you for **taking the trouble** to come here.

1637- あふれる/afureru [v] *overflow, be filled with*

バスタブから水が**あふれる**。
Water is **overflowing** from the bathtub.

1638- 葉/ha [n] *leaf*

秋になり**葉**の色が変わる。
The color of **leaves** changes in the fall.

1639- 種/shu [n] *kind, species*

新しい**種**が見つかりました。
A new **species** has been found.

1640- 迷惑/meiwaku [na-adj] *troublesome, annoying*

大きな音のバイクは迷惑だ。
Loud motorcycles are **annoying**.

1641- つかむ/tsukamu [v] *grab, grasp*

ロープのはしをつかむ。
Grab the end of the rope.

1642- 締める/shimeru [n] *tighten*

ズボンのベルトを締める。
I **tightened** my belt.

1643- ラジオ/rajio [n] *radio*

災害の時はラジオを聴こう。
Listen to the **radio** in the event of a disaster.

1644- じっと/jitto [adv] *still*

猫がじっとしている。
The cat is standing **still**.

1645- うなずく/unazuku [v] *nod*

問いにうなずく。
Nod in response to the question.

1646- 餌/esa [n] *feed, bait*

毎朝、鳥に餌をやる。
I **feed** the birds every morning.

1647- 背中/senaka [n] *back*

背中をマッサージしてほしい。
I would like you to give me a **back** massage.

1648- 両方/ryoohoo [n] *both*

両方のやり方を試す。

Let's try it **both** ways.

1649- 床/yuka [n] *floor*

床に物を置かないように。

Do not leave things on the **floor**.

1650- 囲む/kakomu [v] *surround*

花壇をフェンスで囲む。

Surround the flowerbed with a fence.

1651- 並べる/naraberu [v] *arrange, line up*

きれいに皿を並べる。

Arrange the dishes neatly.

1652- 黙る/damaru [v] *hold one's tongue, to be silent*

叱られると彼は黙る。

He **becomes silent** when he is scolded.

1653- きり/kiri [p] *since, after, end*

電話で話したきり、何も知らせがこない。

I have not heard from him **since** we talked over the phone.

1654- 風景/fuukee [n] *scenery, landscape*

風景の写真を撮った。

I took a picture of the **scenery**.

1655- ごとし/gotoshi [aux] *like, as if*

光陰矢のごとし。

Time flies **like** an arrow.

1656- 保存/hozon (suru) [v] *preserve, store, save*

このデータは必ず**保存**してください。

Please be sure to **save** this data.

1657- 社長/shachoo [n] *company president*

社長になってから忙しい。

I have been busy since I became **president of the company**.

1658- 目立つ/medatsu [v] *stand out*

彼は背が高いので**目立つ**。

He **stands out** because he is tall.

1659- 保護/hogo [n] *protection, preservation*

この寺は**保護**の対象です。

This temple is eligible for **preservation**.

1660- 確実/kakujitsu [na-adj] *certain, sure*

確実な情報がほしい。

I want information that is **certain**.

1661- 経済/keezai [n] *economics, economy, finance*

世界の**経済**の予想を読んだ。

I read about the global **economic** forecast.

1662- 等/nado [suffix] *and so on, etc.*

ご質問やご要望**等**は電話でお問い合わせください。

If you have any questions or requests, **etc**, please contact us by phone.

1663- 演奏/ensoo [n] *musical performance*

高校生のバンド演奏を聴く。

I listened to a **musical performance** by the high school band.

1664- 増やす/fuyasu [v] *increase, add*

株で貯金を増やす。

I will **increase** my assets through the stock market.

1665- 温泉/onsen [n] *hot spring, spa*

温泉でゆっくり過ごしたい。

I would like to relax at a **hot spring**.

1666- 工夫/kufu [n] *devising, figuring out*

工夫された料理がおいしい。

I like cooking that takes a bit of **figuring out**.

1667- 触る/sawaru [v] *touch, feel*

毛皮に触る。

Touch the fur.

1668- 教室/kyooshitsu [n] *classroom*

教室に黒板がある。

There is a blackboard in the **classroom**.

1669- 登録/tooroku [n] *registration, entry*

ショッピングサイトの登録を削除しました。

I deleted my **registration** from the shopping site.

1670- 長さ/nagasa [n] *length*

定規で**長さ**をはかる。

Measure the **length** with a ruler.

1671- 資格/shikaku [n] *qualification, capacity*

弁護士になる**資格**は何ですか。

What is the **qualification** to become a lawyer?

1672- 明確/meekaku [na-adj] *clear, definite*

明確な規定がない。

There are no **clear** rules.

1673- 記載/kisai (suru) [v] *description, mention, record*

詳細は下部に**記載**されています。

The details are **mentioned** at the bottom.

1674- 肌/hada [n] *skin*

赤ちゃんの**肌**にやさしいせっけんを使う。

Use soap that is gentle on your baby's **skin**.

1675- 倒れる/taoreru [v] *fall, collapse*

嵐で木が**倒れる**。

The tree will **fall** in a storm.

1676- 症状/shoojoo [n] *symptom*

インフルエンザの**症状**は何ですか。

What are the **symptoms** of the flu?

1677- 普及/fukyuu [n] *spread, popularization*

インターネットの**普及**が進んでいる。

The popularity of the Internet is **spreading**.

1678- すると/suruto [conj] *then, thereupon*

するとかぼちゃが馬車になった。

Then, the pumpkin turned into a horse carriage.

1679- 優れる/sugureru [v] *be superior, excel, be excellent*

彼女は数学に優れる。

She will **excel** at mathematics.

1680- 返事/henji [n] *answer, reply*

二十四時間以内に返事を送るように。

You must send a **reply** within 24 hours.

1681- 職場/shokuba [n] *workplace*

職場での性別による差別は禁止されている。

Gender discrimination in the **workplace** is prohibited.

1682- 取り出す/toridasu [v] *take out, pick out, retrieve*

必要な情報をデータベースから取り出す。

Retrieve the necessary information from the database.

1683- 骨/hone [n] *bone*

人体には約二百の骨がある。

The human body has about two hundred **bones**.

1684- 平和/heewa [n] *peace, harmony*

世界の平和を願う。

I wish for world **peace**.

1685- 間違い/machigai [n] *mistake, error*

計算に間違いがある。

There is a **mistake** in the calculation.

1686- まい/mai [aux] *sentence end; negative*

二度と同じ間違いはする**まい**。

Never make the same mistake again.

1687- けんか/kenka [n] *fight, quarrel*

兄弟で**けんか**をする。

I had a **fight** with my brother.

1688- 偉い/erai [i-adj] *great*

偉い発明家の伝記を読む。

I am going to read the biography of a **great** inventor.

1689- 熱い/atsui [i-adj] *hot, heated*

熱いアイロンに気をつけて。

Be careful with the **hot** iron.

1690- 当日/toojitsu [n] *that day, current day, the day*

当日に入場券を買う。

Buy an admission ticket on **the day**.

1691- 残り/nokori [n] *rest, remainder*

残りの仕事は明日やろう。

Let's do the **rest** of the work tomorrow.

1692- 支援/shien [n] *support, assistance*

失業者は経済的な**支援**が必要だ。

Unemployed people need financial **assistance**.

1693- 実行/jikkoo [n] *practice, execution*

計画はすでに**実行**中です。

The plan has already been **executed**.

1694- 握る/nigiru [v] *grasp, grip*

テニスラケットを握る。
Grip the tennis racket.

1695- 出会い/deai [n] *meeting, encounter*

出会いのためのサイトに登録する。
I registered with a website for **meeting** people.

1696- 体重/taijuu [n] *body weight*

毎日体重を計ります。
I check my **weight** every day.

1697- 上司/jooshi [n] *boss*

上司の指示に従う。
Follow your **boss**'s instructions.

1698- 結論/ketsuron [n] *conclusion*

結論は先に述べなさい。
Please state your **conclusion** first.

1699- 毛/ke [n] *hair, fur*

ペットの毛がソファについている。
Pet **hair** is stuck to the couch.

1700- テーブル/teeburu [n] *table*

テーブルにお皿を並べてください。
Please arrange the dishes on the **table**.

1701- 盛ん/sakan [na-adj] *popular, prosperous*

この街では漁業が盛んです。

This town is a **prosperous** fishing town.

1702- 急ぐ/isogu [v] *hurry, rush*

帰宅を急ぐ。

I am **hurrying** home.

1703- ともかく/tomokaku [adv] *anyhow, anyway*

ともかく、うまく行った。

Anyway, it went well.

1704- 犯人/hannin [n] *offender, criminal*

犯人がつかまった。

The **criminal** was caught.

1705- 熱/netsu [n] *heat, fever*

風邪で熱がある。

I have a **fever** from a cold.

1706- 犯罪/hanzai [n] *crime*

ネット犯罪が増えている。

Internet **crime** is on the rise.

1707- 批判/hihan [n] *criticism, judgement*

芸術作品は批判の対象です。

Fine artwork is subject to **criticism**.

1708- 出発/shuppatsu [n] *departure*

飛行機の出発の時間が遅れる。

Departure of the flight will be delayed.

1709- 遊び/asobi [n] *playing, play*

ごっこ遊びは幼児期に重要だ。

Pretend **play** is important in early childhood.

1710- 教師/kyooshi [n] *teacher*

数学の教師になりたい。

I want to be a math **teacher**.

1711- 横浜/yokohama [n] *Yokohama*

横浜で観覧車に乗った。

We rode a Ferris wheel in **Yokohama**.

1712- 脳/noo [n] *brain*

脳に刺激を与える。

Stimulate your **brain**.

1713- レストラン/resutoran [n] *restaurant*

新しいフレンチのレストランに行こう。

Let's try the new French **restaurant**.

1714- そろそろ/sorosoro [adv] *soon, any time now*

そろそろ出かけないと遅れるよ。

Leave **soon**, or you will be late.

1715- けが/kega [n] *injury, hurt*

けがのために一ヵ月仕事を休みました。

I took a month off work due to an **injury**.

1716- 兄弟/kyoodai [n] *siblings, brothers*

兄弟が三人います。

I have three **brothers**.

228

1717- 楽器/gakki [n] *musical instrument*

楽器を習いたい。

I would like to learn how to play a **musical instrument**.

1718- 保つ/tamotsu [v] *keep, preserve*

部屋の温度を保つ。

Keep the room temperature steady.

1719- 自動車/jidoosha [n] *automobile, car*

自動車産業は自動運転システムを開発している。

The **automobile** industry is developing self-driving systems.

1720- ほんの/honno [adv] *just, mere, only*

最近ほんの少し暖かくなった。

It has gotten **just** a little warmer lately.

1721- カメラ/kamera [n] *camera*

電話のカメラの写真を掲載する。

I am posting photos from my phone **camera**.

1722- 寺/tera [n] *temple*

寺で除夜の鐘がなる。

The **temple** bells ring on New Year's Eve.

1723- ビデオ/bideo [n] *video*

360度パノラマビデオを撮る。

I am taking a panorama **video**.

1724- 適切/tekisetsu [na-adj] *suitable, proper*

仕事に適切な服を着てください。

You must wear **proper** clothes for the job.

1725- 見事/migoto [na-adj] *excellent, stunning*

花のショーで見事な蘭が展示されている。

Stunning orchids are on display at the flower show.

1726- 底/soko [n] *bottom, sole*

靴の底を張り替える。

I replaced the **sole**s of my shoes.

1727- 刺激/shigeki [n] *stimulation*

赤ちゃんは刺激が必要だ。

Babies need **stimulation**.

1728- 勢い/ikioi [n] *speed, force, momentum*

勢いを維持して！

Keep up the **momentum**!

1729- 吹く/fuku [v] *blow*

台風で強い風が吹く。

A strong wind is **blowing** due to a typhoon.

1730- 迷う/mayou [v] *get lost*

初めてのところで道に迷う。

I have **gotten lost** because it is the first time on these roads.

1731- 背/se [n] *height, stature, back*

背の順に並ぶ。

Line up in the order of **height**.

1732- 生/nama [n] *raw, fresh*

刺身というのは生の魚だ。

Sashimi is a dish comprised of **raw** fish.

230

1733- 訴える/uttaeru [v] *sue, complain*

住民が騒音を**訴える**。

Residents **complain** about the noise.

1734- 精神/seeshin [n] *mind, spirit*

精神と体のバランスを保つ。

Keep your **mind** and body in balance.

1735- 把握/haaku [n] *grasp*

事実を正確に**把握**する。

I have a clear **grasp** of the facts.

1736- 対する/taisuru [v] *face, be in response*

お客さんに**対する**時はおもてなしの心を持つように。

Have second-to-none hospitality in mind when **facing** customers.

1737- 十二/juuni [n] *twelve*

一年には**十二**ヵ月ある。

There are **twelve** months in a year.

1738- 地震/jishin [n] *earthquake*

日本では**地震**がとてもよくあります。

Japan has **earthquakes** very often.

1739- 応援/ooen [n] *support, cheering*

野球チームの**応援**団に参加する。

I am in a group that **supports** the baseball team.

1740- 人類/jinrui [n] *mankind, humanity, human*

科学者は**人類**の進化が早くなっていると言います。

Some scientists say that **human** evolution is accelerating.

1741- 上昇/jooshoo [n] *rising, ascending*

出会い系アプリの人気は上昇の傾向にあります。

The popularity of matchmaking apps is on a **rising** trend.

1742- 空間/kuukan [n] *space, room*

その空間は風水でアレンジされています。

That **space** is designed in accordance with feng shui.

1743- 複雑/fukuzatsu [na-adj] *complex, complicated*

複雑な問題は人口知能に聞こう。

Ask AI to solve **complex** problems.

1744- 特定/tokutee [n] *specific*

特定のスキルのある人材を探しています。

We are looking for people with **specific** skills.

1745- 高める/takameru [v] *raise*

環境問題への意識を高める。

Raise awareness of environmental issues.

1746- 以外/igai [n] *except , other than*

水曜以外で都合のいい日はありますか。

Is there a convenient day **other than** Wednesday?

1747- 観点/kanten [n] *viewpoint*

私たちは違う観点を持っています。

We have different **viewpoints**.

1748- 努める/tsutomeru [v] *make efforts, strive*

任務を遂行するために努める。

I will **strive** to fulfill my mission.

1749- 二時間/nijikan [n] *two hours*

彼女を二時間も待っています。

I have been waiting for her for **two hours**.

1750- きつい/kitsui [i-adj] *hard, tight*

スケジュールがきつい。

My schedule is **tight**.

1751- 祖母/sobo [n] *grandmother*

私は祖母に育てられました。

I was raised by my **grandmother**.

1752- プラス/purasu [n] *plus, benefit*

この資格はあなたにプラスになるよ。

This qualification will be a **benefit** for you.

1753- 大抵/taitee [adv] *usually*

宿題は大抵一時間で終わらせます。

I **usually** finish my homework in an hour.

1754- 狙う/nerau [v] *aim*

的を狙う。

Aim for the target.

1755- 知り合い/shiriai [n] *acquaintance*

知り合いにホリデーカードを送る。

I send holiday cards to some **acquaintances**.

1756- 迫る/semaru [v] *approach*

危険が迫る。

Danger is **approaching**.

1757- どうぞ/doozo [adv] *please*

どうぞこちらにお座りください。
Please sit down here.

1758- 消す/kesu [v] *put out, turn off*

九時に電気を消す。
Turn off the light at nine o'clock.

1759- 唯一/yuiitsu [adv] *only*

魚釣りが唯一の趣味です。
Fishing is my **only** hobby.

1760- 青い/aoi [i-adj] *blue*

今日は青い空がきれいだ。
The **blue** sky is beautiful today.

1761- 終了/shuuryoo [n] *end, termination*

キャンペーンの終了を告げる。
Announce the **end** of the campaign.

1762- をもって/o-motte [cp] *by, with*

勇気をもって、彼は敵と戦った。
With courage, he fought with the enemy.

1763- 前提/zentee [n] *premise, prerequisite*

我々は違う前提で議論をしている。
We are each arguing a different **premise**.

1764- 四つ/yottsu [num] *four*

クローバーは四つ葉があります。
The clover has **four** leaves.

1765- 未来/mirai [n] *the future*

誰も未来はわからない。
No one knows the **future**.

1766- 僕ら/bokura [pron] *we (used by males)*

僕らはみんな生きている。
We are all alive.

1767- 立ち上がる/tachiagaru [v] *stand up*

国家斉唱のために立ち上がる。
Stand up for the national anthem.

1768- 同/doo [n] *the same*

私の住所は同上です。
My address is **the same** as above.

1769- 推移/suii [n] *transition, change*

株式市場の推移を見守る。
I am watching for **changes** in the stock market.

1770- なくす/nakusu [v] *lose something*

子供はよく手袋をなくす。
Children often **lose** their gloves.

1771- 有効/yuukoo [na-adj] *valid, effective*

私の運転免許は来年まで有効です。
My driver's license is **valid** until next year.

1773- 上では/ue-dewa [cp] *on the viewpoint of, according to*

学校の規則の**上では**、携帯電話は使ってはいけません。

According to the school rules, the use of mobile phones is not allowed.

1774- 国内/kokunai [n] *domestic*

今年は**国内**旅行に行きます。

I am going on a **domestic** trip this year.

1775- 都合/tsugoo [adv] *circumstances, convenience*

ミーティングに**都合**のいい場所はどこですか。

Where would be a **convenient** place for a meeting?

1776- 主な/omona [and] *main, important*

主なポイントはウェブサイトに書いてあります。

The **main** points are written on the website.

1777- ふと/futo [adv] *suddenly, casually*

ふと今日の用事を思い出した。

I **suddenly** remembered my errands for today.

1778- 四年/yonen [n] *four years*

学士を取得するのに**四年**かかる。

It takes **four years** to get an undergraduate degree.

1779- 無視/mushi [v] *ignore*

迷惑なコメントは**無視**しましょう。

Let's **ignore** the silly comments.

1780- 一気に/ikkini [adv] *in one gulp, without stopping*

彼は**一気に**ビールを飲んだ。

He drank beer **in one gulp**.

1781- 手続き/tetsuzuki [n] *procedure, process*

運転免許証を更新する**手続き**は何ですか。

What is the **procedure** to renew my driver's license?

1782- 波/nami [n] *wave*

波が砂の城を流してしまいました。

The **wave** washed away the sandcastle.

1783- 仲/naka [n] *relationship*

友達たちの**仲**を取り持つ。

I mediate the **relationship** between my friends.

1784- 中学生/chuugakusee [n] *junior high school student*

今年の春に息子が**中学生**になった。

My son became a **junior high school student** this spring.

1785- イタリア/itaria [n] *Italy*

このバッグは**イタリア**製だ

This bag is made in **Italy**.

1786- のぞく/nozoku [v] *peek, peep*

部屋の中を**のぞく**。

I **peeped** into the room.

1787- 誕生/tanjoo [n] *birth, creation*

新しい命の**誕生**を祝う。

Celebrate the **birth** of a new life.

1788- 汚い/kitanai [i-adj] *dirty, filthy*

汚い手を洗いなさい。

Wash your **dirty** hands.

1789- 畑/hatake [n] *field, plantation*

畑でとうもろこしを育てる。
We raise corn in the **field**.

1790- 履く/haku [v] *put on*

新しい靴を履く。
I **put on** a pair of new shoes.

1791- 膝/hiza [n] *knee*

彼は膝を床につけてプロポーズした。
He proposed with one **knee** on the floor.

1792- 提案/teean [n] *proposal*

上司に提案書を提出しました。
I submitted a **proposal** to my boss.

1793- 業務/gyoomu [n] *business, service, duties*

この車は業務用です。
This car is for **business** use.

1794- 幸い/saiwai [adv] *luckily, fortunately*

幸いに怪我はありませんでした。
Luckily, I did not get injured.

1795- かわいそう/kawaisoo [na-adj] *pitiful, poor*

かわいそうな子犬を拾った。
I took home a **pitiful** puppy.

1796- 画像 gazoo [n] *image, picture*

ショートメッセージで画像を送る。

Send **images** with a short message.

1797- 孫/mago [n] *grandchild*

私には七人の**孫**がいます。

I have seven **grandchildren**.

1798- つなぐ/tsunagu [v] *connect, to tie*

そのアプリは世界中の人々を**つなぐ**。

The app **connects** people around the world.

1799- 包む/ tsutsumu [v] *wrap*

プレゼントをふろしきで**包む**。

Wrap the present with a *furoshiki**.

*Furoshiki is a square piece of cloth used for carrying items or gift wrapping in Japan.

1800- 思い切る/omoikiru [v] *give up, despair*

大学に行く夢を**思い切る**。

I am **giving up** my dream of going to college.

1801- 事態/jitai [n] *situation*

厳しい**事態**だ。

It's a tough **situation**.

1802- 夜中/yonaka [n] *middle of the night*

夜中に目が覚めた。

I woke up in the **middle of the night**.

1803- 改める/aratameru [v] *change, reform*

ロゴを**改める**。

We are **changing** our logo.

1804- 集中(する)/shuuchuu (suru) [v] *concentrate*

読書に集中する。

Concentrate on reading.

1805- 両手/ryoote [n] *both hands*

両手で箱を持つ。

Hold the box with **both hands**.

1806- 指示/shiji [n] *instruction, indication*

次の指示を待ちなさい。

Wait for the next **instruction**.

1807- 結婚式/kekkonshiki [n] *marriage ceremony, wedding*

結婚式を島であげた。

We had our **wedding** on an island.

1808- 虫/mushi [n] *insect, bug*

虫は嫌いです。

I hate **bugs**.

1809- バイク/baiku [n] *motorcycle*

バイクの免許を取った。

I got a **motorcycle** license.

1810- 確立(する)/kakuritsu (suru) [v] *establish*

店の評判を確立する。

Establish a reputation for your store.

1811- 到着/toochaku [n] *arrival*

到着ロビーは二階です。

The **arrival** lobby is on the second floor.

1812- かく/**kaku** [v] *scratch*

虫刺されを**かく**。
Scratch an insect bite.

1813- 痩せる/**yaseru** [v] *to become thin, to lose weight*

結婚式の前に**痩せる**。
I will **lose weight** before the wedding.

1814- 親父/**oyaji** [n] *one's father*

親父と酒を飲む。
I enjoy having a drink with **my father**.

1815- なくてはいけない/**nakutewa-ikenai** [cp] *have to, must*

そうじをし**なくてはいけない**。
I **must** clean up the house.

1816- 試す/**tamesu** [v] *try, attempt*

新しい翻訳アプリを**試す**。
I **try** the new translation app.

1817- 終える/**oeru** [v] *finish, end*

プロジェクトを**終える**。
We will **finish** the project.

1818- 遥か/**haruka** [na-adj] *faraway, far*

遥か向こうに山がある。
The mountains are quite **far** away.

1819- 受験/**juken** [n] *examination, entrance exam*

大学**受験**の勉強をする。
I am studying for a college **entrance exam**.

1820- 医師/ishi [n] *doctor*

医師の指示に従う。

Follow your **doctor**'s instructions.

1821- バンド/bando [n] *band*

音楽バンドをやっています。

I'm in a music **band**.

1822- 体力/tairyoku [n] *physical strength*

体力に自信がない。

I have no confidence in my **physical strength**.

1823- 国家/kokka [n] *country, nation*

国家の歴史を学ぶ。

We learn the history of the **nation**.

1824 - ソフト/sofuto [n] *software*

ソフトをインストールする。

Install some **software**.

1825- 長男/choonan [n] *first-born son*

長男が結婚します。

My **first-born son** is getting married.

1826- さっき/sakki [adv] *a little while ago, just before*

さっきの話は何。

What were you saying **just before**?

1827- ごく/goku [adv] *very, quite*

この薬はごく少量で効く。

This medicine works with only a **very** small amount.

1828- 入力(する)/nyuuryoku (suru) [v] *input, enter*

データベースに住所を入力する。

Enter an address into the database.

1829- 十一/juuichi [n] *eleven*

十一歳はまだティーンエイジャーではない。

Eleven years of age is not yet a teenager.

1830- チャンス/chansu [n] *chance*

チャンスは一度だ。

You only have one chance.

1831- 別れる/wakareru [v] *part, divorce*

彼らは三十年間の結婚生活をもって別れることになった。

They decided to divorce after thirty years of marriage.

1832- 昼間/hiruma [n] *daytime*

昼間だけ保育園で働いています。

I work at a nursery school only during the daytime.

1833- 生産/seesan [n] *production*

生産の拠点を海外に移す。

Move our production base overseas.

1834- 要/yoo [n] main point, in short

要はお客様へのサービスが大事という事だ。

In short, customer service is important.

1835- 収める/osameru [v] pay, dedicate

大学の授業料を収める。

I am paying for my college tuition.

1836- 掃除/sooji [n] cleaning, sweeping

掃除用の新しい洗剤を買った。
I bought a new detergent for **cleaning**.

1837- 強化/kyooka [n] strengthen

建物の土台を強化する。
Strengthen the foundation of the building.

1838- 主婦/shufu [n] housewife

主婦と共働きのどちらがいいかしら。
I wonder which is better, being a **housewife** or having a double income?

1839- 徐々に/jojo-ni [adv] *gradually*

消費税は徐々に上がります。
Consumption tax will **gradually** increase.

1840- メーカー/meekaa [n] *manufacturer*

メーカーに仕様の問い合わせをする。
I am contacting the **manufacturer** about the specifications.

1841- あり得る/arieru [n] *possible, likely*

彼がそう言ったというのはあり得る。
It's **possible** that he said so.

1842- 記す/shirusu [v] *write down, mark*

彼のコメントを議事録に記す。
I **write down** his comment in the meeting minutes.

1843- うわさ/uwasa [n] *gossip, rumor*

近所のうわさを聞く。
I am hearing **gossip** about the neighbor.

1844- 保険/hoken [n] *insurance*

海外旅行**保険**を買います。

I am buying overseas travel **insurance**.

1845- 規制/kisee [n] *regulation, restriction*

事故のために道路に**規制**がある。

There are **restrictions** on the road due to an accident.

1846- もの/mono [p] *indicates reason or excuse*

知らなかったのです**もの**。

I did not know about it.

1847- 感想/kansoo [n] *impressions, thoughts*

映画の**感想**をブログに書く。

I am writing my **thoughts** about the film in my blog.

1848- 左右（する）/sayuu (suru) [v] *influence*

人の意見に**左右**される。

He is easily **influenced** by others.

1849- 促進（する）/sokushin (suru) [v] *promote*

健康を**促進する**サプリを注文した。

I ordered some supplements that **promote** good health.

1850- 景色/keshiki [n] *scenery, landscape*

富士山の**景色**を見る。

View the **scenery** of Mount Fuji.

1851- 味わう/ajiwau [v] *taste, savor*

なべ料理を**味わう**。

Taste the hot pot dishes.

1852- アジア/ajia [n] *Asia*

アジアの人口は増えている。
The population of **Asia** is increasing.

1853- 交流/kooryuu [n] *exchange*

国際交流活動に参加する。
I am participating in an international **exchange** program.

1854- 報道/hoodoo [n] *news, journalism, report*

戦地の報道を読む。
Read a battlefield **report**.

1855- 当初/toosho [n] *at first, initially*

当初は、違う計画だった。
At first, we had a different plan.

1856- インド/indo [n] *India*

インドにはガンジス川がある。
The Ganges River is in **India**.

1857- 観察/kansatsu [n] *observation, survey*

昆虫の観察日誌をつける。
I keep a journal of my **observation** of insects.

1858- 電気/denki [n] *electricity*

LED電球で電気を節約する。
Save **electricity** with LED bulbs.

1859- 癖/kuse [n] *habit, tendency*

悪い癖は直した方がいいよ。
You should fix your bad **habits**.

1860- たいした/taishita [adn] *a big deal*

彼の話はたいしたことはなかった。

His story was not **a big deal**.

1861- あり方/arikata [n] *ideal way, situation, method*

福祉の**あり方**を考える。

Think about the **ideal way** to run our welfare system.

1862- どころか/dokoroka [p] *far from, on the contrary*

それ**どころか**、昼食もまだ食べていない。

On the contrary, I have not eaten lunch yet.

1863- 好み/konomi [n] *liking, taste*

そのファッションは私の**好み**です。

That fashion is to my **taste**.

1864- はまる/hamaru [v] *fit, get into, get stuck*

オンラインのカジノゲームに**はまる**。

I am **getting into** online casino games.

1865- 早速/sassoku [adv] *promptly, immediately*

早速のお返事をありがとうございます。

Thank you for your **prompt** reply.

1866- 支払う/shiharau [v] *pay*

コンビニで電気代を**支払う**。

I **pay** my utility bill at a convenience store.

1867- 市民/shimin [n] *citizen*

市長が**市民**から選ばれた。

The mayor was elected by the **citizens**.

1868- メリット/meritto [n] *advantage, merit*

早期教育のメリットは何。

What are the **advantages** of early childhood education?

1869- 近年/kinnen [n] *in recent years*

近年、国際化が進んでいる。

Globalization has been progressing **in recent years**.

1870- 分かりやすい/wakariyasui [i-adj] *easy to understand*

この説明書は分かりやすい。

The instruction manual is **easy to understand**.

1871- 製品/seehin [n] *product, goods*

新しい製品を開発する。

Develop new **products**.

1872- 果たして/hatashite [adv] *sure enough, as expected*

果たして成功するだろうか。

Would it succeed **as expected**?

1873- 得意/tokui [na-adj] *be good at, be proud at*

あなたの得意な科目は何ですか。

Which subject **are** you **good at**?

1874- 二週間/nishuukan [n] *two weeks*

二週間後にまた来てください。

Please come back in **two weeks**.

1875- 問い合わせ/toiawase [n] *inquiry*

オフィスに問い合わせの手紙を送りました。

I sent a letter of **inquiry** to the office.

1876- あっ/a [interj] *Ah! Oh!*

あっ、ここになくしたイヤリングがあります。

Oh, here is my lost earring.

1877- 何だか/nandaka [adv] *somewhat, somehow*

何だか居心地がよくないなあ。

Somehow, I don't feel comfortable here.

1878- 過程/katee [n] *process*

ここまでの過程をレビューしよう。

Let's review the **process** up to this point.

1879- 仕組み/shikumi [n] *structure, mechanism*

この機械の仕組みを学ぶ。

I am learning how this machine is **structured**.

1880- 慌てる/awateru [v] *be in a hurry, be flustered*

遅刻しそうなので慌てる。

I **am flustered** as I am running late.

1881- ざるを得ない/zaruwo enai [cp] *cannot help doing*

笑わざるを得ない。

I **cannot help** laughing.

1882- 措置/sochi [n] *measure*

一時的な措置を実行する。

We will execute a temporary **measure**.

1883- 油/abura [n] *oil*

油でてんぷらを揚げる。

Fry the tempura in **oil**.

1884- 半年/hantoshi [n] _half a year_

半年に一度のセールだ。

It's a **half-yearly** sale.

1885- 視線/shisen [n] _one's gaze, one's eye_

写真から視線をそらしました。

My eyes moved away from the picture.

1886- 構造/koozoo [n] _structure, construction_

教育の構造改革が求められています。

There is demand for reform in the **structure** of our education system.

1887- 筋肉/kinniku [n] _muscle_

筋肉がつくように運動をする。

I am exercising to build **muscles**.

1888- 少々/shooshoo [adv] _just a minute, for a moment_

少々お待ちください。

Please wait **for a moment**.

1889- 対策/taisaku [n] _measure, counterplan_

外交問題への対策を検討する。

Contemplate a **counterplan** to address foreign affair issues.

1890- 濃い/koi [i-adj] _dark, strong_

濃いお茶を飲んだ。

I had a **strong** tea.

1891- 異常/ijoo [na-adj] _abnormal_

これは異常気象だ。

This is **abnormal** weather.

1892- 図書館/toshokan [n] *library*

図書館で本を借りる。
I am borrowing a book at the **library**.

1893- 靴/kutsu [n] *shoe*

靴をみがきました。
I shined my **shoes**.

1894- おそれ/osore [n] *fear, danger*

洪水のおそれがあります。
There is a **danger** of flooding.

1895- 二階/nikai [n] *second floor*

会議室は二階です。
Our conference room is on the **second floor**.

1896- あえて/aete [adv] *purposely, deliberately*

あえて詳細は省きました。
I **purposely** omitted the details.

1897- 三回/sankai [n] *three times*

週に三回ジムに行きます。
I go to the gym **three times** a week.

1898- 失礼/shitsuree [n] *rudeness, impoliteness*

失礼しました。
Excuse me for my **rudeness**.

1899- 太る/futoru [v] *get fat, gain weight*

毎日ケーキを食べたら太る。
You will **get fat** if you eat cake every day.

1900- いったん/ittan [adv] *for a moment, once*

電話を**いったん**切ってから、かけ直します。

I am going hang up **for a moment** and will call you again.

1901- 取り入れる/toriireru [v] *take in, adopt*

学校が新しいカリキュラムを**取り入れる**。

The school is **adopting** a new curriculum.

1902- モテる/moteru [v] *be popular*

彼は子供に**モテる**。

He **is popular** with children.

1903- 都会/tokai [n] *city*

都会の暮らしはストレスがたまる。

It is stressful living in the **city**.

1904- 大量/tairyoo [na-adj] *large quantity, massive, a lot of*

プリンターが詰まって**大量**の紙を無駄にしてしまった。

I wasted **a lot of** paper because of a printer jam.

1905- 発言/hatsugen [n] *remark*

会議で**発言**をした。

I made some **remarks** at the meeting.

1906- 炒める/itameru [v] *stir-fry*

チキンと野菜を**炒める**。

Stir-fry chicken with vegetables.

1907- 投げる/nageru [v] *throw*

ボールを**投げる**。

Throw the ball.

1908- 玄関/genkan [n] *entrance, front door*

玄関でお客様を出迎える。

We greet our guests at the **front door**.

1909- 一種/isshu [adv] *species, kind, sort*

これも野菜の一種だ。

This is a **kind** of vegetable.

1910- 世代/sedai [n] *generation*

世代が違うと考え方も違う。

Different **generations** have different ways of thinking.

1911- にあたって/ni-atatte [cp] *at the time of, on the occasion of*

入学するにあたって制服を購入してください。

On the occasion of entering your new school, you will need to purchase a school uniform.

1912- 申し込み/mooshikomi [n] *application*

学校への申し込みを送る。

Send the **application** form to school.

1913- 高まる/takamaru [v] *heighten, raise*

期待が高まる。

Our expectations have **been raised**.

1914- 証明/shoomei [n] *proof*

生年月日の証明が必要だ。

I need **proof** of my date of birth.

1915- 沸く/waku [v] *boil*

お湯が沸く。

The water is **boiling**.

1916- 必死/hisshi [na-adj] *desperate*

必死にロープにつかまる。

She is **desperately** holding onto the rope.

1917- 真剣/shinken [na-adj] *serious*

真剣な話を聞く。

I am listening to a **serious** story.

1918- まさか/masaka [adv] *by no means, never*

まさかこんな事になるとは思わなかった。

I **never** thought it would be like this.

1919- ごめんなさい/gomennasai [interj] *I'm sorry, Excuse me*

いじわるを言ってごめんなさい。

I am sorry that I said something so mean.

1920- 画面/gamen [n] *screen*

画面にポップアップボックスが出る。

A pop-up box came up on the **screen**.

1921- 米/kome [n] *rice (uncooked)*

米は生産地によって味が違う。

Rice has a different taste depending on where it grows.

1922- 成果/seeka [n] *result, accomplishment*

努力の成果が現れる。

We are seeing the **result** of the effort.

1923- 物語/monogatari [n] *story, tale*

歴史の物語を読む。

Read an historical **story**.

1924- 日時/nichiji [n] *date and time*

日時が決まったらお知らせします。

I will inform you when the **date and time** have been decided.

1925- 来年/rainen [n] *next year, coming year*

来年のあなたの幸せを祈っています。

I wish you happiness in the **coming year**.

1926- 巻く/maku [v] *wrap up, coil*

寿司をのりで巻く。

Wrap the sushi **up** in a sheet of seaweed.

1927- こっち/kocchi [n] *this way, here*

早くこっちにおいで。

Come **this way** now.

1928- 必ずしも/kanarazushimo [adv] *not necessarily, not always*

必ずしも親のアドバイスが役立つとは言えない。

Parents' advice is **not always** helpful.

1929- たっぷり/tappuri [adv] *plenty*

チキンかつにたっぷりソースをかける。

Put **plenty** of sauce on the chicken katsu.

1930- はやる/hayaru [v] *in fashion, be popular*

ヒップホップ音楽がはやる。

Hip hop music **is popular**.

1931- 恐ろしい/osoroshii [i-adj] *terrible, terrifying*

恐ろしい事件が起こった。
A **terrifying** crime was committed.

1932- 中身/nakami [n] *contents, interior*

はやく箱の中身を見たい。
I can't wait to see the **contents** of the box.

1933- スピード/supiido [n] *speed*

車のスピードの出し過ぎに注意する。
Be careful not to exceed the **speed** limit.

1934- 一歩/ippo [n] *a step*

赤ちゃんが一歩ずつ歩いた。
The baby walked **step** by **step**.

1935- 牛乳/gyuunyuu [n] *(cow's) milk*

牛乳よりも豆乳が好きだ。
I prefer soymilk rather than cow's **milk**.

1936- 否定/hitee [n] *denial*

彼は否定している。
He is in **denial**.

1937- 踏まえる/fumaeru [v] *be based on, have origin in*

前例を踏まえて決める。
It was a decision **based on** previous experiences.

1938- 若干/jakkan [n] *some, few, somewhat*

若干の違いはあるが満足だ。
I am satisfied, although there are **some** differences.

1939- 箱/hako [n] *box*

靴を箱に入れる。
Put your shoes in the **box**.

1940- テニス/tenisu [n] *tennis*

テニスの新しいラケットを買う。
Buy a new **tennis** racket.

1941- アパート/apaato [n] *apartment*

新しいアパートにデポジットを払う。
Pay a deposit for the new **apartment**.

1942- 面接/mensetsu [n] *interview*

仕事の面接で緊張する。
I was nervous at the job **interview**.

1943- 住民/juumin [n] *residents*

区役所で住民登録をする。
Register as a **resident** at the ward office.

1944- て参る*/te-mairu [cp] *go, come, do and come back (humble)*

今日は神社に行って参ります。
I will **go** to the shrine today.
*The phrase "te-mairu" is usually used in its extended polite form of "te-mairimasu".

1945- ギター/gitaa [n] *guitar*

ギターを弾きながら歌う。
Sing as you play the **guitar**.

1946- 要素/yooso [n] *factor, element*

五行では、五つの要素で占う。

Five-element philosophy tells fortunes based on the five **element**s.

1947- 泳ぐ/oyogu [v] *swim*

浮き輪なしで泳ぐ。

I **swim** without a life buoy.

1948- 大勢/oozee [n] *many people, crowd*

大勢の人が初詣に行った。

Many people went to *Hatsumoude**.

*A visit to a shrine on New Year's Day to pray for the health and happiness of their family.

1949- 習慣/shuukan [n] *habit, custom*

朝はコーヒーを飲むのが習慣だ。

I have a **habit** of having a cup of coffee in the morning.

1950- 込める/komeru [v] *load, charge, put into*

おもちゃの拳銃に弾を込める。

Put a bullet **into** the toy gun.

1951- 風邪/kaze [n] *common cold*

風邪をひいた。

I caught a **cold**.

1952- 調整/choosee [n] *adjustment, coordination*

スケジュールの調整が必要だ。

We need to make an **adjustment** to our schedule.

1953- 踊る/odoru [v] *dance*

スタジオで踊る。
I **dance** at the studio.

1954- 遅くとも/osokutomo [adv] *at the latest*.

遅くとも六時までに家に帰らないといけない。
I ought to be home by six at **the latest**.

1955- タクシー/takushii [n] *taxi*

駅からタクシーに乗った。
I took a **taxi** from the station.

1956- 教会/kyookai [n] *church*

その教会は百年以上前に建てられた。
The **church** was built more than one hundred years ago.

1957- 攻撃/koogeki [n] *attack, offence*

軍隊が攻撃を開始する。
The army is starting its **attack**.

1958- 五時/goji [n] *five o'clock*

五時に退社する。
I leave the office at **five o'clock**.

1959- 方達/katatachi [n] *people*

素敵な方達とご一緒した。
I got to spend time with some wonderful people.

259

1960- 久しぶり/hisashiburi [na-adj] *after a long time*

久<small>ひさ</small>しぶりにいとこに会<small>あ</small>う。

I am meeting my cousins **after such a long time** apart.

1961- とたん /totan [n] *as soon as*

「おやつ」と聞<small>き</small>いたとたんに子供<small>こども</small>たちが来<small>く</small>る。

The kids come running **as soon as** they hear the word "snack".

1962- 要する/yoosuru [v] *need, require*

和解<small>わかい</small>には時間<small>じかん</small>を要<small>よう</small>する。

It will **require** time to reach a settlement.

1963- 幅/haba [n] *width, breadth*

額<small>がく</small>の幅<small>はば</small>を測<small>はか</small>る。

Measure the **width** of the picture frame.

1964- 周辺/shuuhen [n] *in the area of, around*

駅<small>えき</small>の周辺<small>しゅうへん</small>には店<small>みせ</small>が多<small>おお</small>い。

There are many shops **around** the station.

1965- 十日/tooka [n] *the tenth day of the month*

電気代<small>でんきだい</small>は毎月<small>まいつき</small>十日<small>とおか</small>が支払日<small>しはらいび</small>です。

My utility bill is due on **the tenth** of every month.

1966- 取得/shutoku [n] *acquisition, get*

運転免許<small>うんてんめんきょ</small>を取得<small>しゅとく</small>する。

I am **getting** my driver's license.

1967- 挑戦/choosen [n] *challenge*

今年はトライアスロンに挑戦します。

I will **challenge** myself with a triathlon this year.

1968- 独立/dokuritsu [v] *be independent*

子供はみんな独立しています。

All my children **are independent**.

1969- 収入/shuunyuu [n] *income, revenue*

収入と共に税金も増えました。

Along with my **income**, my taxes went up as well.

1970- ぜ/ze [p] *sentence end; emphasis*

早く行こうぜ。

Let's go now!

1971- 市場/ichiba [n] *market*

市場は毎朝五時に開きます。

The **market** opens at five o'clock in the morning.

1972- 着物/kimono [n] *kimono*

女性は成人式に着物を着ます。

Girls wear **kimono** for the coming of age ceremony.

1973- メニュー/menyuu [n] *menu*

レストランでメニューを見る。

Look at the **menu** at the restaurant.

1974- 夏休み/natsuyasumi [n] *summer break, summer vacation*

夏休みはどこかに行きますか。
Are you going anywhere for **summer vacation**?

1975- 壊す/kowasu [v] *break, destroy*

彼女はうっかりお皿を壊した。
She accidentally **broke** the dishes.

1976- なさる /nasaru [v] *do (honorific)*

おばあさんが生け花をなさる。
The elderly lady is **making** a flower arrangement.

1977- 仮/kari [n] *temporary, provisional*

仮の家に住む。
I am living in **temporary** housing.

1978- かえって/kaette [adv] *rather, on the contrary*

かえって物事を悪くした。
On the contrary, it made the things worse.

1979- 関する/kansuru [n] *concerning, be related*

税金に関する相談は会計士に連絡する。
Contact your accountant **concerning** your taxes.

1980- 輸入/yunyuu [n] *import*

輸入品店を始めたい。
I want to start an **imported** goods store.

1981- 満たす/mitasu [v] *satisfy, fulfill, fill*

風呂の湯を満たす。
Fill the bathtub with warm water.

1982- いわば /iwaba [adv] *so to speak*

いわば、これが私たちの集大成です。

This is our crowning achievement, **so to speak**.

1983- スタッフ/sutaffu [n] *staff*

テーマパークの**スタッフ**が忙しそうにしている。

The theme park's **staff** seem to be busy.

1984- 住所/juusho [n] *address*

宛先の**住所**を教えてください。

Please provide your mailing **address**.

1985- 平気/heeki [na-adj] *calmness, composure, unconcerned*

迷子になっても彼は**平気**だった。

Even when he was lost, he looked **unconcerned**.

1986- コース/koosu [n] *course*

ゴルフの**コース**を回る。

Go around the golf **course**.

1987- 訪ねる/tazuneru [v] *visit*

昔の友達を**訪ねる**。

I am **visiting** my old friends.

1988- 鍵/kagi [n] *key, lock*

また家の**鍵**を無くしてしまった。

I lost my house **key** again.

1989- 世界中/sekai-juu [n] *around the world*

世界中の人々と友達になりたい。

I want to make friends with people from **around the world**.

1990- 下手/heta [na-adj] *unskillful, poor, clumsy*

彼は掃除が下手だ。

He is **poor** at cleaning.

1991- 詩/shi [n] *poem*

日記の代わりに詩を書く。

I write **poems** instead of a daily journal.

1992- 経過/keeka [n] *passage, progress*

手術後の経過はどうですか。

How is his **progress** after the surgery?

1993- 整える/totonoeru [v] *put in order, adjust, prepare*

客室を整える。

Prepare the guest room.

1994- ツアー /tsuaa [n] *tour*

バスツアーで奈良に行きます。

We are going on a bus **tour** to *Nara**.

*Nara is an ancient city in Japan known for its Daibutsu (Buddha).

1995- 西/nishi [n] *west*

太陽は西に沈む。

The sun sets in the **west**.

1996- 事項/jikoo [n] *matter, item, facts*

質問事項をまとめる。

Summarize the **items** being questioned.

1997- 塾/juku [n] *cram school, tutoring school*

放^{ほう}課^か後^ごに塾^{じゅく}に通^{かよ}っています。

I go to a **cram school** after my regular school.

1998- 去る/saru [v] *leave, go away, pass*

今^{いま}の会^{かい}社^{しゃ}を去^さることにした。

I have decided to **leave** the company.

1999- 五人/gonin [n] *five people*

五^ご人^{にん}が夕^{ゆう}食^{しょく}の席^{せき}に一^{いっ}緒^{しょ}に座^{すわ}りました。

Five people sat together at the dinner table.

2000- 入り口 /iriguchi [n] *entrance*

入^いり口^{ぐち}はどこですか。

Where is the **entrance**?

CONCLUSION

The Japanese language is classified as one of the most difficult languages to learn for English speakers. That is not only because the grammatical structures are so different from the Western languages, but there are also many variations and irregularities in Japanese expressions. That is perhaps because Japanese has adapted elements of both Eastern and Western languages and cultures, and it has evolved as its own language within an isolated island nation. English is indeed one of the languages that has the most influence on modern Japanese. Some words like click, link, door, team, member, etc. have the same meaning as the original English, while others like stress, check, or class only carry a part of their meaning. Those borrowed foreign words are written in katakana and you might have noticed that there are so many borrowed English words in the 2000 phrases introduced here.

Japanese words can be funny in the way that they are made by connecting two or three words. For example, flip phones are sometimes called Garakei. This is a combination of the "Galapagos" islands and "keitai" (portable phone). When smartphones were becoming mainstream, flip phones were loaded with functions that were only compatible with the network system in Japan. They were like animals that evolved on the isolated Galapagos islands, so people started calling flip phones "Garakei".

At the same time, many Japanese words have been used in Western culture as well. Sushi, sake, karate and karaoke have been around for decades. Newer additions are kawaii, bento, emoji, and manga, to name a few. By the way, kara-te (empty hands) and kara-oke (empty orchestra) share the same sound of kara (empty). You can use it for expressions like "my wallet is kara" (I don't have any cash) or "the fridge is kara" (There is no food in the fridge).

Anime is a word altered from animation as it is easier for Japanese people to pronounce. However, outside Japan Anime means the Japanese style of animation. In Japan, anime means any animated film regardless of its origin.

Here are some tips for boosting your Japanese fluency.

- Increase your exposure to the Japanese language. Exposure is the key to learning any foreign language. That goes for Japanese as well. You can increase your exposure to Japanese by subscribing to a Japanese cable channel, watching YouTube videos, or reading Japanese material.
- Build confidence in listening comprehension. If you are a beginner and would like to get started on listening, children's programs are helpful. The distinctive difference between pronunciations in the Western language and Japanese is the use of vowels. Japanese words have a vowel in each sound. K in Book is pronounced as ku. Also, there is no distinctive difference between L or R. L in Table is Ru. A person's first name Laura would sound Roora. As words are spoken slowly and clearly in children's programs, it would be easier for you to decode each sound. Children's songs with lyrics are also a good place to start. With illustrations or animations, it is easier to absorb the meanings.
- Challenge yourself by reading a wide range of topics. If you are an intermediate learner and would like to go one step further than hiragana, reading a newspaper for children, "Kodomo Shinbun", is helpful. Intended for middle to upper grades in elementary school, it includes hiragana for advanced kanji characters. Yet, topics include current national

and international events as well as academic topics like science. You may find many of the words in this book and the level matches with JLPT.

- Interact with native speakers. Some of the chat apps with a live video feature are a good place to meet and interact with Japanese people. With hand gestures and facial expressions, it is not that hard to communicate.

Languages continue to evolve by the people who use them. You are one of the people who will influence Japanese. Count how many Japanese words you use today. How about Tofu for your salad, and add Umami to your soup? Maybe Mochi for dessert!

Enjoy your Japanese! Ja, mata!